The Golf Widow's *Revenge*

PATRICIA JEAN SMITH

CONTEMPORARY
BOOKS, INC.
CHICAGO ■ NEW YORK

Library of Congress Cataloging-in-Publication Data

Smith, Patricia Jean.
   The golf widow's revenge.

   1. Golf—Anecdotes, facetiae, satire, etc.   I. Title.
GV967.S65   1986   796.352'0207   86-29291
ISBN 0-8092-4802-6

Published by Contemporary Books, Inc.
180 North Michigan Avenue, Chicago, Illinois 60601
Manufactured in the United States of America
International Standard Book Number: 0-8092-4802-6

Published simultaneously in Canada by Beaverbooks, Ltd.
195 Allstate Parkway, Valleywood Business Park
Markham, Ontario L3R 4T8 Canada

To
my family,
Ron, Nicole, Owen

Contents

A' are guid lasses, but where do a' the ill wives come frae?

Scottish Proverb

Chapter 1
Doctor's Advice

Physicians, of all men, are most happy; whatever good success soever they have, the world proclaimeth; and what faults they commit, the earth covereth.

Francis Quarles

When my husband's doctor advised him to take up golf, I was an innocent twenty-five-year-old, a bride of three years, still glowing from the honeymoon and still in possession of most of my romantic illusions about the dynamics of marital relationships. Poor, bonny lass that I was, I believed in the fairy tales of my childhood: I believed in the power of the love of young maidens; I believed they could turn beasts into princes, marry them, and live happily ever after. I lived in an Edenic daze in which I often lay naked with my husband and was not ashamed. It seemed to me that on three years' trial marriage could indeed be happy ever after. Little did I know that with a bit of well-intentioned advice from our doctor my Eden would slip away from me as certainly as Eve's and that I would find myself henceforth banished to a world of knowledge, misery, pain, and death, where a woman's work is never done and a golf widow's never ends.

If I had known then of the irrevocable changes the game of golf would make in the character and attitudes of my young husband—that I would witness the transformation of my delightful Don into my demented Don—if I had known then of the murderous thoughts I would come to harbour, I might have shrieked from the top of Vancouver Island's Mount Chimo, "Physician, heal thyself!" But I was "young and easy under the apple bough." The year was 1972. I was twenty-five and innocent—innocent of golf.

I was not, however, ignorant of the game. I had seen it played on television while I was still a child. I had watched Sam Snead sink sixty-foot putts. I could identify Julius Boros and Don January by the age of ten. I learned to recognize a golf ball. I became familiar with the shape of the golf club. As a youngster I would have been able to select a putter from a bag of clubs and describe its use. I understood that there were different types of clubs for different types of shots and that some had wooden heads and that some didn't. Of the many and various wooden heads to be found in the clubhouse I remained ignorant, being at that time too young to partake of alcoholic beverages; nor did I dream of the primitive rites that passed within the holy place; nor did I spend my days in sweet reveries of the many and various uses for the golf club as an instrument of torture.

Thanks to television, I became aware that there is a proper manner for holding a golf club, called the *grip*; a proper stance for hitting the ball, called the *address*; and I learned that the motion by which a golfer addresses his ball and then hits it is termed his *swing*. I did not then know that grips, stances, addresses, and swings could furnish the avid golfer with enough conversational material to last a lifetime, nor did I then know that the golf swing and the unnatural contortions it demands have become a technique for behavioural conditioning of which Pavlov himself would be proud. Had I known the depths of depravity to which the grown man can sink upon his addiction to the game of golf, I might well have adjusted my stance, gripped Don's shoulders, and addressed him with a swing of the old-fashioned sort before the start of his first round of golf. I should have gone a few rounds with him right then. Too late I learned the wisdom of the proverb—if you hang a thief when he's young, he'll no steal when he's auld. Little did I know that it's too late to cast anchor when the ship is on the rocks.

On the television I spied new landmarks termed *fairways* and *greens*. I discovered that a stick, called the *pin*, marked the location of a tiny hole in each green. I noted that on his first shot on each hole the golfer was permitted to place his ball on a small, wooden, nail-like device called a *tee*, thereby elevating the ball and theoretically facilitating a good first shot. Would that the only tee I had come to know was the tea you drink. Little did I dream the day would come when I would long to stick a few pins of my own into a little dummy fashioned in Don's likeness.

I learned that *par* referred to the optimum number of swings, called *strokes*, it should take the golfer to hit his ball off the tee, down the fairway, and into the hole in the green. I understood that par differs from hole to hole, that a complete round of golf constitutes eighteen holes, and that par for the course equals the total of the pars for each hole. I did not know that shooting a round of par golf would become the most dearly cherished goal of Don's life. Little did I suspect that Snead would supplant Shakespeare or that *Golf Digest* would become his new *Bible*.

I heard the terms *rough*, *hook*, and *slice* used in new ways, and I gleaned evidence to suggest that if one were to hook or to slice one would likely end up in the rough, and that if one's ball were to land in the rough his chances of making par would go down. Now when I ponder the depths to which Don's single-mindedness plunged I realize I might have knocked him back on course.

Such was the extent of the theoretical knowledge of the game I gleaned in my childhood. Thanks to television, I became familiar with the rudiments of the game. The havoc it can wreak in marriage I had yet to experience. I had no crystal ball to show domestic scenes in which my husband, arriving home late and exhausted after a day of desultory play, would limp into the kitchen, his ankle twisted from tripping over a tricycle, his neck askew from breaking his fall in the diaper wash on the clothesline, and, after reposing on the sofa and not receiving a beer for his efforts, would scream, "I'm going to get a young wife!" Nor could I have foretold my defiant shriek from the changing table in the nursery, "Good, I could sure use her."

Innocent that I was, I thought that golf was a game like any other, for I had also played it as a child. Following the principle of "Monkey see, monkey do," my brother, my friends, and I had devised a game of our own, an improvisation of the theme we had seen played on the television. Our equipment we borrowed from our parents. Our course was of our own devising. Sprung fresh from the font of our green imaginations, it encompassed holes and hazards unequaled in the modern game: sandboxes, swings, monkey bars, teeter-totters, gravel pits, riverbeds, cattleyards, snake pits, and mountainsides. At the command "Go" we broke from the gate, and, as in any other reasonable game, the object was to finish first.

Yet golf did not become for any of us an exclusive pastime, nor did it become the subject of our deepest hopes and fears. We still went boating, swimming, fishing, water-skiing, and climbing. We retained our curiosity about the world around us, and, had we lived near a paved road, we would, no doubt, have devised a form of tennis. Golf was merely one of the many activities that made life sweeter. Wee bairn that I was, I was left with many pleasant memories of camaraderie and fun. Among the most pleasant were those of warm starlit evenings, moonlight on the lake, the smell of sagebrush and freshly mown grass, the sound of crickets and sprinklers as backdrop for leisurely strolls across the playing fields, golf club and ball in hand, a commentator by one's side speaking in hushed tones into a microphone held to the lips, discussing the highlights of the evening's brilliant play.

Such was my early initiation into the kingdom of golf. I had no inkling of the life that lay ahead. I had not yet started to think of men as sex objects. I had no thought that anatomy could be destiny. I did not suspect that gender could create a gap. Little did I know that golf widowhood would become or could become the Western equivalent of the Mahatma's *sva raj*. I had no warning that the heroics of the golf widow must equal the feats of the legendary *fakir* lying on his bed of nails or walking on his path of burning coals. I had no hint that marriage to a golfer could involve a mental and spiritual discipline unequaled this side of the Himalayas. Little did I know that in middle age, when the girth is wont to spread and the mind is easily cast adrift, my husband would still hearken to dreams of another Gold Trail and be willing to spend all of *our* gold in pursuit of his master's teaching. Would that he had known that though Nature cures the patient, the doctor pockets the fee. Alas, thanks to the halcyon days of my youth, I had been left with a favourable disposition towards the game of golf and, even worse, an open mind on the subject.

Chapter 2

Joint Membership *or* Two Can Play This Game

During our courtship Don expressed the view that marriage was a partnership of equals. He also declared that he wanted to be a writer, dwell in exotic lands, speak foreign languages fluently, rear two or three children, savour fine wines, and prepare *haute cuisine*, while reforming and revolutionizing outmoded economic systems and listening to *Tanzmusik der Praetorius-Zeit*. Instantly I perceived that here was a man of vision to whom destiny had drawn me, and on May 1, 1969, we were married.

For three years there were no omens to portend that our game plan would change. We left the secure world of Vancouver and traveled to England, making our way inland to the wilds of Leeds and dwelling in that far outpost of civilization for one year. Here Don wrote a thesis, huddled at a rickety table next to a perpetually dying coke fire in the wind tunnel that served as our sitting room. While the north wind jet-streamed out of Scandinavia, across the Yorkshire moors, through our eastern window sashes and out our western, thereby getting up steam for onslaughts on Ireland, I prepared bangers and mash in the closet that passed for our kitchen. As the moisture in the air condensed in rivers on the walls, I was kept busy feeding the NeverBright gas meter hard-earned pennies to keep the feeble flames on the elements flickering. When the rains came *silin' doun*, we would quaff our pints of John Smith's Double Brown and hail to each other from behind our mufflers.

"Artee a' rite, luv?"

"Nay, luv. I be rite chuffed off."

In like fashion we spent the first three years of our marriage, and, if you count the year of our courtship during which we maintained separate addresses and Don did his own laundry, we enjoyed each other for a total of four pre-golf years. In those days *Match of the Day* meant a football game or, as we over here in the colonies would say, a soccer game. Getting a master's degree meant receiving a diploma from a university, not winning a green jacket at Augusta National. When we went walking, we went hand in hand, and I did

14

not have to walk ten paces behind so I could check out his backswing while he took practice shots with an imaginary one-iron.

We even spent two weeks touring Scotland, chancing only once on some men in tweeds carrying clubs, or sticks of some sort, who were trudging through sand and heather, pushing aside sheep and sheep droppings, to a spot of green where some white balls were lying. We stopped the car for a moment to deduce what the *daft boogers* were doing. Upon perceiving that they were golfing, we started the car and turned our gaze to the surf from the Sea of the Hebrides and to the seals on the rocks. We continued on, going where fancy and romance beckoned—Loch Lomond, Loch Ness, Mallaig, and Skye. Saint Andrews, that revered and sacred shrine, golf's ancestral home, was only a dot on a map.

Now the Scots have always seemed a hardy, independent, democratic, and intelligent race to me. In fact, I was née a Murdoch, albeit into that branch of the clan that came to the New World shortly after Erik the Red. Granted the Scots wear skirts, play bagpipes, and eat haggis, but even so I find it difficult to believe that they should be credited with the invention of the game of golf in its modern form.

There is evidence to suggest that the Romans

15

played a game appropriately named *paganica* with a leather ball stuffed with feathers and bent sticks for clubs. Therefore, it is possible that some of the legionnaires could have taken the game with them to the outer edges of the known world, to the savages beyond Hadrian's Wall. Possibly the Dutch were to blame. They had early commercial relations with Scotland and played a game called *kolven* on the frozen canals with clubs,

balls, and a stake for putting at. Some have suggested that the east window of Gloucester Cathedral pictures a figure strongly evocative of a golfer. Nonetheless, the Roman Empire collapsed, and with the legionnaires out golfing it is not surprising. Consequently, Italy is no longer famous for her championship courses. The Dutch sensibly concentrated on tulips and cheese while the ancient Britons were more concerned with keeping down the Druids than chasing balls with sticks. So it is the Scots who must take the blame.

I believe that even in Scotland the game would have died out had it not been for the persistence of Scottish legislators. Any novice student of Taoism knows that the best way to encourage something is to forbid it, and this the canny Scots did to golf repeatedly. In March 1497, Parliament decreed and ordained that:

> *wapenshawings be halden by the lordis and baronis spirituale and temporale, four times in the zeir: and that futeball and golfe be utterly cryit doun and nocht usit; and that bowemerkis be maid at ilk paroch kirk a pair of buttis, and schuttin be usit ilk Sunday.*

In 1471 the *wapenshawings* themselves were

forbidden because *"futeball and golfe be abusit in tyme cuming."* Twenty years later another edict was issued by James IV, who is known as the first official Royal and Ancient Patron of the game, since it was in his reign that the Lord High Treasurer of Scotland first entered debits for golf balls. Ironically, his decree read:

> *Futeball and golfe forbidden. Item, it is statut and ordainit that in na place of the realme there be usit futeball, golfe or other sik unprofitabill sportis.*

These royal decrees were followed by similar prohibitions by local councils against the abuse and profanation of the Sabbath, although some councils later acknowledged defeat by reducing the prohibition to the *"tyme of sermons onlye."*

I cannot quarrel with the substance and perspicacity of these statutes. Any bill that orders that golf *"be utterly cryit doun and nocht usit"* gets my vote, and phrases that call the game a *"sik unprofitabill sportis"* are music to my ears. I do not quarrel with the wisdom of the wording or with the intent of the legislation. I question only the tactic of prohibition. Had these ancient lawmakers had the good sense to outlaw *bowemerkis*, Scotland would be a nation of archers today, and every arrowsmith would be gainfully employed.

In time Don acquired a master's degree from Leeds, and we returned to Vancouver. Here he obtained a Ph.D. in English literature, and we settled on the lee side of Vancouver Island, where he could earn some money at a small community college to repay our student loans. Thus it came to pass that he paid that fateful visit to the local physician who advised him to take up golf.

Dr. Gavin McMurdo is a Scotsman. He is also a member of the town's golf and country club. When he thinks a patient needs exercise, he naturally thinks of golf. He even thinks of golf when a patient doesn't need exercise. In short, he spends a lot of time thinking about golf. Once he gets the scent of the heather up, visions of mashies and cleeks, baffies and niblicks start dancing in his head, and his enthusiasm becomes infectious—a veritable health hazard.

"Hae ye nae thought a' golf, lad?"

"No, Doctor, I haven't."

"Well, lad, it's hie time ye did. There's nae thing in this whirled ta compare wi'it. Until ye've golfed, man, ye hae na lived!"

Whereupon Don speeded to the clubhouse of the Chimo Golf and Country Club and took out a joint membership, promising that our partnership could continue on the golf course.

Now I understand that many partnerships are formed on a golf course and that many are terminated. I even understand that there are those for whom golf is secondary to the partnerships they might make on the course. Of the business transactions that take place between tee and green I am ignorant. I know nothing of mergers, corporate takeovers, preferred stock, common stock, deferred debentures, bonds, or the international banking conspiracy. For that matter, neither does Tom Watson. He has E. F. Hutton look after his financial affairs. His other affairs he likes to handle himself. No. My area of specialization has become the avid golfer, the man who converts to the sport. In 1972, conversion experiences and religious fervour were subjects I had some intellectual knowledge of, having just received a Master of Arts degree in religious studies. Yet, at the precise moment at which I was congratulating myself for having completed my education, it was really only beginning.

True it is that hindsight is a great teacher, that well done is twice done, that a bad dog never sees the wolf, that an ounce of practice is worth a pound of preaching, and that you shouldn't speak Arabic in the house of a Moor. It is also true that hindsight is not foresight and that you can't turn back the clock. If only I had known that the man

I married would be irrevocably transformed with one stroke of the club, I might have pleaded with him to try jogging, mountain climbing, skiing, basketball, hang gliding, stock car racing, karate, tennis, kick boxing, or roller derby. Alas, in my innocence I sanctioned the membership and even looked forward to playing golf on a real golf course. Thus, it being hard to put old heads on young shoulders, feather by feather my goose was plucked, and, like a lamb to the slaughter, I was led to the first tee.

Over the years I have been made to understand by the golfers I have known that the secret of the game has been pinpointed as being as many different things as there have been pins to point at by pinpointers, and that one must not confuse this with pin placement, which is an entirely separate discipline. However, there is one attribute that all pandits applaud. In order to play the game, one must *relax*. According to the immortal Snead, when he hits the ball, "my mind is blank and my body is loose as a goose." Now I would have thought that the number of blank-minded golfers would be legion. However, I cannot recall seeing many who could be described as being as loose as a goose. Perhaps too many recall the tragic fate of Goosey Loosey, who was eaten by Foxy Loxy. Perhaps it is because the goose egg, that dreaded

21

score in all other games, cannot be laid on a golf course. If it could, it would no doubt be hit promptly by some poor lout who had mistaken it for his ball.

First of all, the golfer must relax. In no other game is this quite so crucial. Yet, second of all and just as important, the golfer must concentrate. He must be physically relaxed and mentally alert, thereby producing a mind/body dichotomy that Descartes would have envied. So we come to the first logical conundrum of the game. One must be both relaxed and concentrated at the same time.

The second logical conundrum is found in a series of infinite regress, which results in a series of infinite rounds of golf. Again I quote the master, Snead:

> You need desire to play golf—but you need to keep playing the game to maintain the desire. That's something worth thinking about, no matter how old you are, or what you shoot.

Put another way, golfers are always going in circles, which they describe as *playing a round* and which they experience as *playing around.*

Such reflection was far from my mind the sunny afternoon Don turned our 1966 Chevrolet Bel-Air into the parking lot of the Chimo Golf and Country Club. While I was noting how few '66 Chevs there were in the parking lot, he was happy in the knowledge that he would soon be escorting me 'round his newly found Elysian fields. Here he could demonstrate his exceptional natural aptitude for this most demanding of all *sportis*. Alas, what was to transpire could not have been further from his game plan.

Now a golf club is not a place where I feel at home and at ease. I cannot relax in the lounge chairs with the easy grace of the well-established member. Try as I might, I cannot get his open-legged, hunch-shouldered slouch quite right, not even when I have the correct number of beer glasses in front of me. In the pro shop the merchandise is strange to me. I ignore the golf bags and clubs altogether. I cannot recognize the labels in the sweaters or the strange markings on the pockets of the sport shirts. I don't understand why the hats have holes in them, why they sell only one glove and not two, or why the shoes need spikes, particularly when these are not permitted in the clubhouse. I am intimidated by signs announcing "Members and Guests Only," even when I am a member.

In short, when I go into a golf club I get jangled. The sight of the pro shop jangles me. The sight of the clubhouse jangles me. The sight of the course itself jangles me. The announcements that come over the pro shop public address jangle me. The very clubs in my bag jangle me. The moment I step between the yellow markers of the women's tee, place a ball down, and try to hit it, I become an irresponsible idiot.

My throat goes dry. My knees start to shake. My arms turn to wood. I stand there in the awful knowledge that for the moment of the address I am naked at the centre of the world. I can sense that the people in the pro shop are watching. I know that the golfers in the lineup to tee off are watching, though they casually pretend to be loosening up. I can feel the eyes of my fellow players burning into my back. I note the ducks on the water hazard surfacing to see the shot, the willows turning for a better view. The clouds cease scudding. The evergreens surround me. The sky breaks open, and the sun focuses his spotlight. Nature holds her breath. Big Brother is nothing compared to this. By this point I cannot see the ball, let alone hit it.

Such was the state of my mind and body that September afternoon when Don decided to introduce me to the delights of golf. I do not recall whether I hit the ball off the first tee or not. I only recall that my game degenerated into a ruthless repetition of hit and run, hit and run, until at last arriving on a green I would putt with all the finesse of a gorilla. Ten putts were nothing for me.

At first Don was encouraging.

Trish ©

"Don't worry about it, darling. Just try to relax and watch how I do it. Note my easy backswing. See how gently I slap the ball and note my full follow-through. My legs are slightly bent, and my eyes on the ball at all times."

"No, dear. You're not listening to me. Look how you've lined up. You're headed straight for the rough."

"You dumb broad. I told you you were pointing the wrong way. Now watch me."

"Damn! I sliced it. If you'd pay more attention to what I'm saying, we'd be doing much better. Pull yourself together."

"Where's your ball? What do you mean you don't know where it went? Weren't you watching it?"

"Where's my ball? What do you mean you don't know where it went? You stupid expletive-deleted female dog. You also have to watch your playing partner's ball."

"Aren't you listening to me?"

"YOU'RE NOT LISTENING TO ME."

Three hours later we emerged from the bush by the ninth green, red-faced and red-necked. We were no longer speaking. I had had the grim satisfaction of seeing his play descend to my level. I was even convinced that two could play this game, but not together.

Chapter 3

Diapers for Me— Golf Tees for Thee

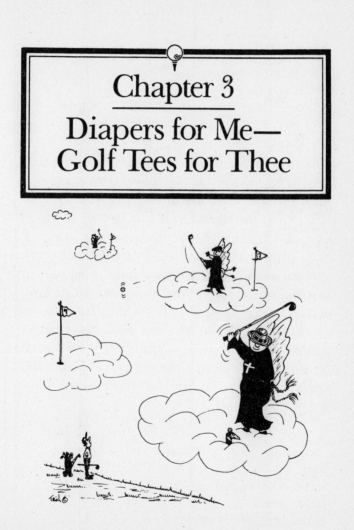

The trouble about reaching the age of ninety-two, which I did last October, is that regrets for a misspent life are bound to creep in, and whenever you see me with a furrowed brow you can be sure that what is on my mind is the thought that if only I had taken up golf earlier and devoted my whole time to it instead of fooling about writing stories and things, I might have got my handicap down to under eighteen. If only they had put a putter in my hands when I was four and taught me the use of the various clubs, who knows what heights I might not have reached.

P. G. Wodehouse
The Golf Omnibus

When Don became a member of the Chimo Golf and Country Club, he was only twenty-nine. He was too young to have regrets about a misspent life, and he was too young for a midlife crisis. He was young enough to become a good golfer, but he was already too old ever to hit the Gold Trail.

At a literal level, the Gold Trail refers to a succession of tournaments held throughout the United States that are open only to a select group of men (and a few women) who have received a card from the PGA, or Professional Golfers Association. Non-Tour professional golfers and amateur golfers are usually forbidden to enter the Gold Trail tournaments, unless the tournament is an Open and not the usual Closed. The sponsors of these tournaments offer large purses of gold to the winners. Any man who fails to win enough of the gold while out on the trail has his card taken away and is immediately banished to Alaska, where he must pan for sufficient gold to buy back his card. This gold is then returned to the sponsors' purses, and in such fashion the bags are kept filled.

Members of the PGA golf to live.

They must golf to eat.

They are mortal men.

On a nonliteral or mythological level, the Gold Trail is the idealized, heavenly realm the ordinary golfer may only dream of entering. The men who have access to it form the priesthood of golf. They have been set apart from and above the rest of mortal golfers, who cannot golf to live but who live to golf. The players on the Gold Trail are wandering mendicants, holy men in quest of perfect golf shots. They are immortal, and their names come down to us in hushed tones through the centuries.

Old Tom.

Young Tom.

Seamus McDuff.

Varden.

Snead.

Smith.

Jones.

The holiness and sacredness of the proceedings at a Gold Trail golf tournament are immediately evident from the strict division maintained between the spectators and the priests. It is obvious in the reverent and hushed tones of the commentators before a priest strikes a ball. And it is obvious from the widespread sale of holy relics.

A holy relic is a piece of golfing equipment that has been blessed by a priest. The priest's name then appears on the equipment, thereby making it a holy object whose magic power will be conferred on any ordinary golfer who might purchase such equipment. Thus, even though the ordinary golfer is denied entrance to the Gold Trail, he may share in the sanctity of the event through the purchase of holy relics. He may then go golfing in the knowledge that blessed are his socks, blessed are his shoes, blessed is his shirt, and blessed are his pants. Similarly, blessed is his bag, blessed are his clubs, and blessed are his balls. Thus, when he hits one of the blessed things like one of the blessed priests, he experiences *Nirvana*.

When Don joined the Chimo Golf and Country Club, he had never heard of the Gold Trail or dreamt of treading upon its holy haunts. He was merely in need of some exercise and had been advised by his doctor that golf was the *"verra potion to gar him great."* Little did he know that this advice was to change the course of his life. To be fair, I must admit that Don did not convert to the game on the first swing that he took at the ball. I believe it was his one hundred seventh, or that swing where the novice hits the sweet spot on his ball and executes a proper golf shot.

There is nothing natural about the execution of the proper golf swing. I assert this despite the thousands of poor sods who have devoted their lives to the perfection of the motion and who earn their living through the perpetuation of the lie that the proper golf swing is a graceful, effortless action. On the contrary, the golf swing is unnatural and, when executed properly, dangerous.

I suspect that some unexplained perverseness in their temperament caused the Scots deliberately to make the game as difficult and unnatural as possible. Perhaps it comes from living too long too close to the English. Perhaps it comes from too long an association with the game itself. However, the consequences of this perversity have had effects far beyond those envisioned by the game's creators. Although I lack scientific documentation for my claim, my own observation of the sport causes me to suspect that the peculiar rotation of the body, in conjunction with the static position of the head that the ideal golf swing demands, affects the brain and central nervous system in such a way as to produce a conversion experience. After the completion of a proper golf swing the brain is unnaturally susceptible to an identification with the flight of the ball as it soars in an arc through the air, which a ball is wont to do if it is hit "properly." Although the ball lands, the novice does not. He remains on some permanent "high," buoyed up by the certainty that if only he had taken the game up soon enough he could have played golf like a priest. His brain is washed clean, to be filled only with golf. From that moment on, a man, like my Don for instance, becomes an avid golfer and is lost to normal life forever.

Similarly, there comes a moment in a female's life when she is lost to normal life forever. The moment is termed *childbirth*. From this moment on, the female loses her physical and mental freedom, and her destiny irrevocably parts company from that of the male. For her there is no more carefree jumping on her bike and going for a ride unless she first changes the baby's diaper and packs up the diaper bag—complete with change mat, diapers, plastic pants, bottles, baby food and spoon, Handi-wipes, and teething ring. Then she must put on the infant carrier seat and helmet and buckle in the babe. For her there is even no more carefree walking out of doors unless she first changes the baby's diaper and packs up the diaper bag—complete with change mat, diapers, plastic pants, bottles, baby food and spoon, Handi-wipes, and teething ring. Then she must assemble the stroller and buckle in the babe or put in the car seat and buckle in the babe. No more traveling light. The new mother has a new crib, but she can have no more cribbage in the Chimo Hotel with a few friends and a couple of cool ones. They do not allow infants in such establishments even when the newborn is completely concealed in a Snuggli. A quick-witted waiter, ever alert for crime and corruption, will, nine times out of ten, spot the encased baby and soon put the run on the mom.

"What you got in there, lady?"

"In where?"

"In that green pouch you've got strapped to your chest."

"In here? Why, a stuffed puppy dog, of course."

"Stuffed puppy dogs don't cry like a baby, lady."

"This is a talking stuffed puppy dog. It has a

string that you pull out if you want it to say 'Mama.' "

"Look, lady, the RCMP will be making their rounds soon, and I ain't going to get my license revoked by permitting minors on the premises. Get your act together and get the two of you out of here before I boot you out. Move it. Now."

It is touching scenes like this one that have given motherhood a bad name. Today, however, more women seem to know of the abuse they might have to take by giving birth and are joining the army instead.

By contrast, I grew up in a traditional household where the father or titular head of the family went out and earned the living while the mother stayed home and provided it. Consequently, it was not unusual that I should have held the notion, quaint as it is now deemed, that children do best when reared with a twenty-four-hour, seven-day-a-week, one-to-one relationship known as a *mother*.

I do not mean to imply that the birth of our daughter was an occasion for anything other than celebration. On the contrary, in these days of planned parenthood it is comforting to know that there is still room for the occasional miracle. However, our daughter's birth, coinciding as it did with Don's conversion to golf, meant a parting of the ways unforeseen in the early days of our partnership. It is impossible for a young mother to breast-feed while putting or to squeeze eighteen holes of golf in between naps. Our joint membership in the club ended.

As I was initiated into the mysteries of formula, feeding, burping, and schedules, Don was pondering the secrets of driving, chipping, and putting. While I was discovering how to care for the navel, give the daily bath, and assemble a diaper bag, Don was busy learning how to fade, how to draw, and how to assemble a golf bag. While I was acquiring a crib, baby bath, high chair, walker, and stroller, Don was purchasing a new golf bag, clubs, glove, balls, tees, and umbrella—all suitably blessed. When I was worried about constipation, rashes, diarrhea, thumb sucking, and measles, he was worried about hooks, slices, blisters, sunburn, and thunder. When I was preoccupied with toilet training, he was perfecting his short game. While I attended birthday parties and preschool, he attended interclubs and stag night, and our lives proceeded upon separate but parallel lines.

Chapter 4
Stag Night

Our sport loving ancestors from which [sic]
we have inherited the game of golf evidently
never intended that it should be more than an
idle pastime, as surely there was no science in
knocking a piece of wood around the ice by
the early Dutch in Holland nor could any
thing but fun, a mere passing of the time, be
attached to the pleasure that the shepherds
on the Scotch [sic] hills had in hitting a little
pebble from one place to another with their
shepherds' crook.

As golf has come down through the years
we have been inclined to make more work
out of it and less play. We have, without
serious intent made a science out of the
ancient pastime, each generation contribut-
ing its bit.

With the development of the golf clubs
and links on which we play it has become a
game of skill which has today reached its
highest perfection. So as a science it must be
treated so [sic] if we are to accept it se-
riously—and few there are who do not take
the game in a serious way.

H. B. Martin
What's Wrong with Your Game? (1928)

One of my earliest observations about avid golfers was the fact of the dead seriousness with which they approach the game of golf. To an outsider they seem as incapable of poking fun at themselves in the pursuit of their *sportis* as Jehovah's Witnesses are of poking fun at their religion. However, I have come to see that among the initiated there is room for a modicum of levity in the ritual telling of the golf joke. This is done under the tightly controlled conditions of the nineteenth hole in the clubhouse. Indeed, I have occasionally overheard some lighthearted banter being exchanged between members on the practice greens. One golfing wit whom I observed even pretended to be out practicing his bad shots in order to give his comrades a chance to earn some of their money back. Yet once out on the course itself, the serious scientists emerge, and propriety and decorum ideally rule the play. And when a nongolfer suggests that there is something daft about the pursuit of a little, white ball over such a long distance, the reaction of the avid golfer is cool, if not downright acidic.

Initially, the severity of these reactions seemed peculiar, for I was not then enlightened to the religious fervour the game inspires and the spiritual torment the avid golfer endures. I thought of him as a sport-loving man, a mere innocent shepherd.

When Don started playing the game, most of our friends thought of the golfer not as a shepherd, but rather as a wolf in sheep's clothing, in spite of the fact that sheepskin would violate the dress code of every club in North America. In those days many of our contemporaries were just recovering from a prolonged bout of Beatlemania complicated by the industrial/military complex. For them golf conjured up images of rotund, middle-aged, affluent, male members of the Establishment. To admit to being a golfer was tantamount to taking personal responsibility for the war in Vietnam, the death of Che, and the spread of capitalist imperialism. Consequently, the reaction of many of our friends to Don's golf was disbelief, followed by shock, followed by disbelief, followed by derision. First they would attack the game on the political grounds outlined above. Next they would object to the senseless nature of the game itself and question its exercise quotient. Finally they would make their objections purely particular. Don was simply too young to golf. To all of these gibes and attacks Don was impervious. His brain had already been washed clean, and he continued playing.

At the time I felt that a partial explanation for Don's marked change in behaviour might come from the circumstance that his formative years had fallen during the late fifties and early sixties—that any fan of the Big Bopper or Bill Haley and the Comets might theoretically run the risk of becoming a golfer. Alas, the true cause was more serious. The effect of the golf swing had begun its insidious work on his nervous system and cerebral cortex. His handicap had already slipped below the maximum thirty-six allowable and had dipped to thirty-three. His enthusiasm for the game was whetted.

Before Don took up golf he was unable to get out of bed before ten o'clock in the morning. By ten he was able to raise his head from the pillows and make a few tentative movements in his lower members. Eleven o'clock was prime time. At this hour all his extremities cooperated willingly, and he was able to remove the bed covers and arise for brunch. It was not uncommon to find him still abed and asleep past noon. Once or twice he went fishing, but in preference to waking at dawn he would stay up all night and go to bed when the tide washed him ashore. Those of us who knew and loved him avoided disturbing him with an early morning telephone call. The harsh bells of the telephone vibrated at precisely the correct frequency to turn our Sleeping Beauty into a Beast. As a young golfer he preferred an early afternoon tee time, but as the novice graduated, his times got earlier and earlier. His behaviour markedly changed, and within a year he could make an 8:00 A.M. start.

There is a misconception about, to which I have already alluded, that golf clubs are bastions of the wealthy and the privileged—that one must join the elite before joining the club. This is simply not true. The example of our local club puts the lie to this error at once. Up and down the island the Chimo Golf and Country Club is known in its brother establishments as the "Lunch Bucket Club." Their brother golfers have put their fingers on the obvious statistic that a high percentage of Chimo Club members work at the Chimo Pulp and Paper Mill. The suggestion is that the Chimo Club lets in the riffraff. The truth lies elsewhere.

To play golf a man must have a lot of free time during the daylight hours. He must have more than a lot. He must have plenty. This central fact has been obscured by the predominant number of clubs that have raised their initiation fees so high that the average Joe cannot afford to join. Consequently, the misconception abounds that in order to golf a man must have plenty of money, when in reality all he needs is plenty of time. This is the one characteristic that unites all golfers—the former president and the lad on the green chain; the simple shepherd on the Scottish hillside and the simple corporate executive at GM. They all have the time it takes to play a round.

From what I have been able to observe over the years, a decent game of golf requires a minimum of six hours. Playing the full eighteen holes usually takes four hours in the summer, when the course is habitually busy. In the fall and winter the keen golfer can expedite a round in three. However, if the course is packed or if he has the bad luck to find himself behind a tournament of Kiwanis members or a tournament of Nissan dealers, for example, the round itself may take the keen golfer six hours and leave him in an agitated frame of mind. This is why the serious player prefers an early tee time. It gives him a head start on the pack. On an average day six hours is enough for the whole thing. It allows a man time for travel to and from the course. It accommodates a few putts on the practice greens and a number of full swings to loosen up. It gives the golfer time to leave the humdrum world behind and allows him a few moments for quiet contemplation of the lofty play ahead. He has sufficient leisure to savour the delusion that his best round lies before him and to experience the mental exhilaration that this thought engenders. Finally, it gives him the time he needs after the day's play to recuperate in the clubhouse and analyze what went wrong.

Plenty of time is the essential requirement for golf. That is why a job that requires shift work is the ideal occupation for the man who lives to golf. If a man is working graveyard, he can go straight to the course from work; if he is working afternoons, he can go straight to work from the course. The only shift that is problematical is the day shift, but since it occurs only one shift in three and since there are usually two days off between shifts, employment at the Chimo Pulp and Paper Mill is strongly favoured by avid golfers.

Chimo sits socioeconomically with those parts of Canada which hew wood, draw water, and make profits—all for export—and which are collectively referred to as "Middle Canada." However, unlike the rest of Middle Canada, Chimo sits geographically in the one spot in the country where it is possible to play golf all year 'round. As a nation we are currently infamous for our hockey players. Nonetheless, if global climatic conditions were to change dramatically, making the northern climes less icy, the shift work patterns of a large percentage of Canadian males would be ideal for the nurturing of avid golfers. And who knows what mutations would thereby arise in the game's evolution?

Although Don did not and does not work at the mill, he was able to enjoy the same amount of free time during the daytime as the mill worker through the clever manipulation of his college timetable. By volunteering to teach night courses on "The Thematic Concerns of the 20th Century Prose Epic" in Horsefly and Moosejaw, he was able to leave most of his days free for golf. This arrangement was particularly agreeable to his colleagues, none of whom shared his affliction and all of whom disliked traveling long distances at night.

Plenty of time is the prime requirement for

playing golf. The paradox of the game is that while it takes three to four hours to play a round it takes only two seconds to make a golf shot. If one allowed a golfer ninety-five shots for the completion of a hypothetical round, he would spend a mere three minutes making golf shots. In four hours on the course he would actually get in only three minutes of golf. The rest of the time his mind would be free to wander, and he would have ample time after one shot to worry about his next.

Golf requires an inordinate amount of time for a single game but, paradoxically, permits only a minute amount of actual playing time. This is fine for shepherds, who have their sheep to count, but it wreaks havoc with the golfer, who has only his shots to count. The better a golfer gets, the fewer shots he has to count; but the less time he takes making shots, the more time he needs to play to keep in form. He needs to spend more time on the course, which in turn gives him more time to think about his shots. Thus there comes a moment in a golfer's life when the second ingredient that he needs to keep playing the game is plenty of nerve.

Golf gives a man time to think. It gives him time to be alone with his thoughts. It compounds the strain on the nervous system that the proper golf swing requires with an inordinate amount of time to think between shots, and thinking is not something that comes easily to golfers. Some get the shakes and are unable to putt. Some get the shakes and are unable to drive. Some get the shakes and are unable to walk and prefer to drive; hence the increasing popularity of the golf cart. Some just shake. Some spend a lot of time in the clubhouse buying their nerve at the bar before emerging on the course. Others spend a lot of time in the clubhouse buying it back. Golf wreaks havoc with the nervous system, and if it were not for the weekly institution of Stag Night, there might well be no men fit for the game at all.

In 1928, H. B. Martin observed that "there are hundreds of first-class golfers in America, any one of them with the ability to win a championship, but without the necessary nerve to put forth his best efforts at the crucial moments." I surmise that what has changed the course of golfing history is the institution of Stag Night in North American golf clubs.

Stag Night gives golfers a weekly vent for their frustrations. It soothes their overtaxed brains. It lets them get back their nerve. Stag Night is the time when the scientists kick up their hooves. As soon as a whining, cowering creature slithers up the paved walkway from the eighteenth green, his nerve broken by the day's play, he is lassoed by the pro and his assistants and put in a pen in the bowels of the clubhouse. At the end of the week, when the pen is full, the pro opens the gates, and his assistants give the hysterical creatures a pair of antlers to put on. They are then permitted upstairs to partake in the Stag Night festivities. During these weekly celebrations the broken golfer becomes a changed being. Here he gives up his clubs and puts on his horns. Here he can relax in the company of his fellow stags, imbibe copious quantities of stag juice, and sink his teeth into moose steak. Here he is free to drink as much juice as he needs, without being bothered by any of the does. Here he may simply sit and watch the other stags at cards, at dice, or at pool. He may, if he chooses, enter into the play himself and place friendly wagers with the other stags. He is even free to shake his antlers and prance about, and if he is feeling particularly frisky, he may paw the carpet and charge the other stags. However, since this usually leads to a locking of horns and broken antlers, these antics are generally frowned on by most stags. At the end of such an evening the golfer's spirits are renewed. He is loose as a goose and eager for another round.

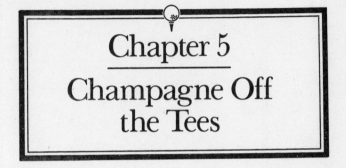

Chapter 5

Champagne Off
the Tees

One sunny Sunday in July at 6:56 A.M. in the year of Our Lord, One Thousand Nine Hundred and Seventy-Nine, the residents in the upper-middle-class houses in the quality subdivisions surrounding the Chimo Golf and Country Club were startled out of their collective slumbers by the sound of gunfire. Miniature explosions were coming from every tee on the course, but it was not the usual shotgun start. The geese were fleeing the water hazards, and the terror in their honks and the rush of their wings could be heard above the shaked roofs by the panic-stricken inhabitants within.

Mothers ran to secure their children to their bosoms while fathers speculated whether or not the tensions inherent in the game had finally led to open warfare on the tees. Would a scene of carnage and bloodshed of astonishing proportions meet their purview? they wondered. They rushed to their windows and threw open their sashes. And what to their wondering eyes should appear? Not a miniature sleigh and eight tiny reindeer but hundreds of golfers raising their beer!

Their eyes, how they twinkled! Their dimples, how merry! Their cheeks were like roses, their noses like cherries. But in place of their beer they held clutched in their hands not bottles, but goblets instead. And with a wink of their eyes and a nod of their heads they soon let the dads know there was nothing to dread. So they drew in their shutters and went straight back to bed.

At a meeting held the week before, the Match and Handicap Committee of the Chimo Golf and Country Club decided that it was time, once and for all, to rid the club of its lunch bucket connotations. Although lunch buckets were no longer permitted on the course, the stigma had remained, and they had suffered from it long enough. It was, therefore, important to make a lasting impression on their brother golfers from the hallowed Rusty Oaks Club of Victoria in the upcoming interclub. Consequently, the members present at the meeting decided to start the day by serving champagne off the tees. Not only would they serve it off the first tee, but they would serve it off every tee on the course. They would have it bubbling out of the water fountains on the sixth, eleventh, and seventeenth holes. They would have it issuing from the water faucets in the locker rooms and gurgling from the showers. They would have drained the water hazards and filled them with the stuff too had the cost not been prohibitive, so they settled for the less expensive option of emptying a number of bottles around the course and letting the bubbly settle in little pools of casual water. No one would ever again be able to imply that the Chimo Club didn't go first class.

Such was the committee's intent. And indeed it was a day that made a lasting impression on the members from Rusty Oaks. Some later claimed that, while they had little or no recollection of the play and no idea of how they had gotten home, their impressions of the match lasted for days and, in some cases, for weeks afterward.

There is a side to the game of golf that is epitomized by the links at Rusty Oaks. While golf may have at one time been the preserve of Scottish shepherds, the history of the game took a dramatic shift with the union of England and Scotland under the reign of James the Sixth of Scotland, better known as James the First of Great Britain and Ireland. In 1603, when the crowns of the two countries were united on one head, it became fashionable for English aristocrats, ever on the lookout for new means of occupying their time, to take up golf and establish exclusive clubs for their private pursuit of the *sportis*. Given the length of time necessitated for a round of golf, it was enthusiastically embraced by the aristocrats. The game received the apellation Royal and Ancient, and soon the distinct ambience that only an aristocrat can impart came wafting across the links. Large, regal castles called *clubhouses* were constructed by large, regal architects. Spires, bars, turrets, banquet halls, ballrooms, guestrooms, water closets, dressing rooms, and stables were mandatory. Hardwood oak floors, hand-carved sideboards, banquet tables, crystal chandeliers, silver tea services, silver dinnerware, portraits of the members done in oils and framed in gold, plush carpets, embroidered cushions, silk sheets, and Irish linen—all became part of the new ambience on the links. Large, regal gardens were incorporated into the course by large, regal landscape architects. The greens now were manicured. Little lakes, fountains, rills, and bridges were conceived to refresh the patrons' spirits and enhance the setting. What nature had forgotten the servants remembered, for the sensitive, aristocratic soul survives only through the tender nurture of a vast entourage of valets, waiters, chefs, butlers, grooms, stable boys, errand boys, chambermaids, and gardeners. Within a trice the game was transformed and enriched by all the ambience in which an aristocrat is born. As an afterthought, little sheds were erected in back of the castles for the golfing instructor and the golfing gear.

The first impression that a golfer has of Victoria's Rusty Oaks, as he approaches the course from Ocean Drive, is that this is a club in which the very finest golfing traditions have been well preserved. Even the members look well preserved. Here, the golfer senses, is a place where every desire, every need, every whim has been anticipated, every thought taken care of. This is a place set apart from the rat race. Rats are simply not allowed, and while betting remains a royal art, rat races are forbidden.

As the golfer turns his automobile onto the expansive oak-lined avenue from which the club takes its name, he knows that here nothing is left to chance. Nature is artfully incorporated into each vista. Rhododendrons, camellia bushes, azaleas, roses, hollyhocks, and lady's slippers line the

bridle paths. Each hole features some unique panorama or some famous golfing hazard— Golfer's Gulch, Loser's Leap, the Hangman's

Hole, Quagmire Reach, the Haunted Woods, Heart Attack Hollow. And the drama of the approach to the clubhouse is unparalleled this side of the Atlantic. From the moment the golfer steps out of his motor carriage and hands the reins to the groom, he knows that he has left the mundane behind. As he watches the stable boy lead his car to its box stall and give it a nose bag of oats, he knows he has entered the realm of the Royal and Ancient.

Would His Highness like to reserve a cart?

Will His Worship be requiring the services of a caddie?

Would Your Grace like to take some refreshment in the clubhouse before commencing his round?

Perhaps Milord would care for another little bit of *pâté de fois gras*? Another snifter of brandy?

If I might suggest, Sire, many of the members here prefer to spend a few moments in the sauna or have the masseuse give them a good rubdown before commencing their round. They find it helps them to get loose as a goose quickly, thereby improving their score. Or perhaps you would prefer to wait and sauna after your round?

Would Your Grace permit us to shine his shoes or press his suit?

Perhaps Your Worship would care to avail

himself of some more refreshment in the privacy of the Men's Lounge off the dressing rooms?

Horrors, Sir! No one mentions money here. It's just not done. If I may be so bold, Excellency, I should inform you that no silver may touch the palm at Rusty Oaks. It's considered degrading to speak of it, an insult to one's breeding. Just sign on the dotted line, if you would be so good, Sire.

Rusty Oaks is a club for all seasons. One visit gives a man an appreciation of the enthusiasm of the members for breakfasting at the club, dining at the club, entertaining at the club, or putting up one's guests at the club so that one doesn't have to put up with them at home. The members of Rusty Oaks know that their club stands for a tradition to which they might lack the title but a tradition to which they are deservedly entitled. You can hear this assurance in their voices as they chide their entourage. You can measure it in the expansion of their chests as they survey the course from the flagstone steps of the pro shop. One glance assures any onlooker that the members of Rusty Oaks are well steeped in ambience—an ambience that is not lost on the lunch bucket set.

Chapter 6
Return to the Links

There comes a day in every golf widow's life when she realizes that her husband's attraction to the game of golf is more than just a passing fancy, more than a phase that he will grow out of. There comes a time when she has still not faced up to the truth of her situation, but she is beginning to suspect that something is amiss. If her spouse had merely been out sowing wild oats, the crops would have produced a bumper yield; the hay loft would be full and the silos overflowing. Out in the fields the stooks would be rotting and all the mice feasting. Yet where has the farmer been through all this? Out golfing? Thus there comes a time when the widow's credulity wears a little thin, when she concludes that this attraction to the inane pursuit of a little, white ball has gotten out of hand and that she had better get out to the pasture herself to see what the devil is going on. Consequently, in the summer of '79, I made the judicious decision to return to the links.

This decision was facilitated by the fortuitous arrival of my mother in Chimo. She was anxious to spend a lot of time with her sole grandchild, who had by now reached the civilized age of four, and I was guilt-free knowing my daughter's education and upbringing were in competent hands. For the first time since the early years of our marriage I had sufficient time to golf.

I also had sufficient incentive. I would not claim that I was suffering from a broken heart from Don's neglect. The pain I felt was more like a nagging wound—serious but not debilitating. Yet the sore could not heal in face of the daily proof that Don's mania for the game was not waning but rather waxing and that I was rapidly losing touch with him. Golf is, after all, not a contact sport. Our parallel lines had curved and had not crossed. If Don were put to the Royal and Ancient Acid Test and asked in what order he would give up his family, his estates, and his club, I feared I already knew the truth. Perhaps out on the course we might again find some common ground.

On a more practical level, I was forced to renew

my membership in the Chimo Club because I was
no longer able to follow Don's conversation. I no
longer knew what he was talking about. The avid
golfer is not satisfied with merely playing the
game as often as he can get his hands on his clubs.
He is compelled to add insult to injury by replay-
ing the thing orally as if to assure his wife that
there is no other woman in his life and that he
can account for every moment of his time. He
gives her a detailed account of his game to prove,
beyond a shadow of a doubt, that he has been
playing a round and not playing around. But how
could I know what he was doing if I couldn't
understand what he was saying? How could I
know if he had been where he'd said he'd been if
I hadn't been there myself? He was talking about
parts of the course that I had never seen—the
fairways and the greens. For all I knew, the road
for the landscape machinery might cross the seventh fairway and not the first, as he claimed. How
did I know that crossing the road with your first
drive was to complete a wondrous golf shot? Was
it really possible to land in the water hazard on
eighteen on your second shot? Could one truly go
out of bounds off the tee at thirteen? Why was it
bad luck to have to take a drop on ten? What was
wrong with three-putting five greens?

I had gleaned from his descriptions of his games that his handicap was now down to seventeen and that this was good, very good.

Did I know how few players out of all the men and women who had ever lifted a club from the beginning of time had ever broken ninety?

Ninety clubs?

No, you idiot! Ninety strokes.

No, I didn't.

About ten percent! That's how many!

I could tell from the triumphant tone in his voice that breaking ninety was one of the high points in a golfer's career. However, I still had trouble reconciling this with his admiration for the men who could shoot their age. Don was only thirty-six. By this scheme of reckoning he still had a long, long way to go. What could it all mean?

Furthermore, he had started entering tournaments: match play, medal play, the two-man-best-balls, the three-ball match, the two-man tag team, the four-man-best-balls, and the intersquad. He began winning prizes, useful domestic items such as an icebox, a kerosene barbecue, a pair of trinoculars, and an electric bug zapper. He started to bring home trophies and began to get his picture in the *Chimo Times*. He was becoming a local celebrity while I was still trying to fathom the meaning of the term *porch climber* or the affectionate diminutive *porchie*.

Don was methodically working his way into the inner circles of the golfing set. He was now noticed by men with handicaps of five or six. They invited him to make up foursomes. They offered him the chance to make a little money. They encouraged him to press.

Some pandits take the attitude that if you can't beat them you should join them. Personally, I've always preferred to beat them. I know it's not ladylike, but I like to win. I like to beat Don every chance I get, and it was becoming obvious to me that if I were ever going to beat him on the golf course I had better hurry up and join him. And, as if this were not incentive enough, Don had begun to drop little Zen koans such as "What will we do in our old age if you don't golf?"

Clearly the time had come to dust off my golf clubs. The Fates were cooperating. The Oracle was showing the way. Therefore, knowing that what's good for the gander is sauce for the goose and what's good for the bee is good for the hive, I descended the stairs to the root cellar to retrieve my clubs. Wondering what's the good of a sundial in the shade, what's the good of a pipe if it's not played on, I reached for my golf bag. It was an antique model from Scotland, circa 1922, with a three-cornered tear in the canvas, just above the ball pouch. I selected a driver, a spoon, a brassie, and a baffy. Then I added a cleek, all of my mashies, two niblicks, and my favourite putter. After some consideration I chose three leather balls, a couple of gutties, and a few "bounding billies." However, just to be certain, I added some Hogans and went back up the stairs.

As I was loading my clubs into the trunk of our 1966 Chevrolet Bel-Air, I did pause to reflect on the power of the Zen koan in preventing rational thought. Nevertheless, I shrugged off my doubts, reminding myself that who never climbs will never *fa'*. Besides, I was becoming increasingly concerned that our daughter was growing up with a warped vision of reality. She was adamant in her opinion that Daddies worked at golf clubs, and I knew that she was too young to be persuaded otherwise. Perhaps the best thing was to compound her confusion by demonstrating that Mommies could work there, too.

At this phase of his golfing career Don had reached the point where it was no longer cool to be seen golfing with one's wife, except in the cooler part of the day, during the twilight hours, when a man is all fagged out from the real thing but still has the leisure and inclination for an evening stroll with his spouse. And just to add a little more interest to the outing, why not hit a few balls as well? By this time she should have finished her chores, and a night out might do her some good. Consequently, the Chimo Club has adopted the institution of twilight golf. They have set aside a time at which a stag may properly be seen in the company of his doe. If he is seen golfing in her company at any other time, he is liable to be put off his game by friendly shouts from fellow stags on neighbouring fairways, inquiring if the old lady is out showing him how it should be done, or asking if he is picking up any good pointers. Chortle. Chortle. I have yet to see a stag who takes kindly to chortling. One chortle from a fellow stag will throw a golfer off his game. Two chortles and he is just as likely to start breaking clubs. The only time a chortle is acceptable is on Thursday evenings during the summer months when the members and their does set out on their evening stroll. Consequently, twilight golf has become a popular institution at the club, and the practice of husband and wife making up a team has an archaic charm that appeals to the lovers of all that is Royal and Ancient. First the husband hits the ball and then the wife. They proceed taking alternate turns until one team member holes out. At the next hole the process is reversed: the wife hits the ball off the tee, and her husband is forced to make their recovery. This sort of sport appeals to the wife, too. She has the unique satisfaction of watching her husband take half the blame for their round, and she has the added enjoyment of knowing that at the end of nine holes she may partake of a meal she has not had to cook.

However, as I set out for the Chimo Golf and Country Club that sunny summer morning I had no thought for, or any appreciation of, the charms of twilight golf. I was out for the real thing, too. I would show Don how the game should be played, but I had a lot of lost time to make up for, approximately five years. I had given Don a five-year head start. If I were ever going to beat him at his chosen game, the only grass I could henceforth allow to grow under my feet was the tender blades of greenery out on the course.

For the next few weeks I devoted myself to the mastery of the game with a passionate and single-minded determination. I was oblivious to everything except the progress of the little, white ball I was following that day. I was oblivious to the four-car collision that occurred on the highway

that parallels the first fairway and that, I was later instructed by the RCMP, must have coincided with my approach shot to the green. I was oblivious to the brush fire on eight and the lightning that had ignited it. I was later told that the only reason I had lived to golf again was the fact that I had been wearing running shoes. Since that day I have always worn running shoes when playing the eighth hole. I carry a pair tied to my bag and put them on before I tee off. When I reach the ninth hole I change back to my regular footgear. In the best golfing tradition I was oblivious to everything but my little, white ball. Only nightfall deterred me.

Initially, I was even oblivious to the pain in my upper arms, which was getting more severe each day. Had I not been trying to make up for Don's five-year head start, I might have sensed that something was wrong, that perhaps I should take it a little easier. In order to make up for my late start I had calculated that I had to get in fifty-four holes a day for the next three months. I ignored the pain and continued playing, knowing that after thirty-six holes I would cease to notice it. It was not until the pain became so severe that I could not raise my arms above my shoulders without fainting that I called it quits. After a mere three weeks I was back at home licking new wounds and nursing a grudging respect for the game and the men who play it.

In retrospect, however, I have perceived that not everyone can golf. Some of us are not fit for it. Try as we might, we cannot be blank-minded. Somewhere along the way we have acquired the habit of thinking and cannot stop. By contrast, the men who take to the game immediately must needs be naturally blank-minded. They have never acquired the habit of thought.

As I have suggested, the golf swing is an unnatural and dangerous motion, particularly for those whose minds are full, for those to whom thinking comes naturally. The properly performed golf swing causes the neck to coil, and the pain of the strangulation thus induced must have somewhere to go. In those whose minds are full, the pain cannot go up. It must go down to lodge in some other part of the body. In my case it was the upper arms that suffered. Some find the pain is wont to settle in their back, while some find their knees tend to give out, and in a few isolated instances the pain will lodge in the foot. However, in the case of those who have never acquired the habit of thought, the head is empty and the pain may rise up. It goes to the head where it is not noticed. In fact, I speculate that, while it may not be noticed by the avid golfer, the pain activates an electromagnetic current in the cerebral cortex that catalyzes the conversion experience, causing a momentary blackout and subsequent memory loss. The only thing the avid golfer knows when he recovers from his swing is that he was born to golf and that if only he had started soon enough he could have played the game like a priest.

My determination to play the game like a priestess lasted three weeks. I was forced to give up golf once more, but not because of the injuries I suffered on the course. Not because of my arms. Six months of physiotherapy healed them. No, a closer examination of my physical condition caused our family physician to conclude that I was pregnant again.

Chapter 7
Sunday Blues

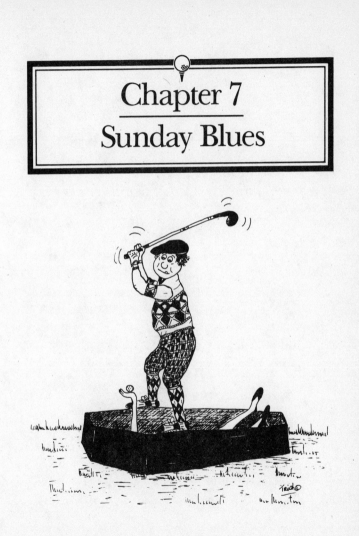

Every time Mommy joins the golf club she gets pregnant. Now Daddy won't let her play anymore.

Although this statement was never wholly accurate, the coincidence of the two events—my joining the Chimo Club and my subsequent pregnancies—made a good story that Don was fond of recounting and our daughter was fond of repeating. It is now a canonical part of our family mythology.

In fact, the birth of our son in 1980 had nothing to do with my second futile stab at golf. Our daughter had begun to query why it was that she did not have a brother or a sister. And we were getting old enough to know that if she were ever going to have one we had better hurry up and plan a pregnancy.

Before the birth of our son I often commented that one child takes up all of a mother's time; therefore, she might as well have two. While there is a modicum of truth in that statement, the parent of one child has no conception of what it is like to be the parent of two. She has no conception of the true meaning and full import of the phrase *sibling rivalry*. While one child has only its parents to argue with, two children may argue with each other. This situation is infinitely better for the children because neither of them ever tires of the game, unlike parents, who tire quickly. When a mother has only one child, she finds herself in a one-to-one relationship in which the odds are equal. There are even times when the dad comes home and backs her up. At such times the odds are two to one in her favour. However, once she has her second child, a mother finds herself outnumbered, with odds of two to one against. Even when the dad comes home, the best that she can hope for is two to two. Thus, even when the odds are evened, the best that she can hope for is a fifty percent chance of coming out ahead. While the mother of one may naively assume that one and one make two in straightforward arithmetic progression, the mother of two discovers that the addition of another child presents a geometric progression for which she was not prepared. The addition of a second child causes a quantum leap that could not be foreseen.

In such an altered situation a woman may find

that opinions she once espoused with ease are liable to change. She may give up her illusions about the nobility of motherhood, seeing an advantage to full-time day care that she had never before been able to appreciate. She may come to realize that the more people to whom her child is exposed during its formative years can only be for the good—the child learning to adapt to new situations and new ground rules, thereby enhancing its early awareness and making a brighter child, one more able to adapt easily to a rapidly changing world. She may even find that wage slavery and the regimentation of a nine-to-five job have charms that heretofore were lost upon her. She may go back to work. Or she may find that there is no work for her to go back to.

I, for one, never seriously considered the possibility of returning to work after the birth of our son. Those who pursue a degree in religious studies have little illusion of securing a place in the work force upon the completion of their degree. The best that they may hope for is to found a cult of their own someday. And in my case that option was also out of the question since I had embraced the time-honoured institution of motherhood. If I were to found a cult, it would have to be after the chicks had flown the coop.

Besides, I had more than enough work to do at home, particularly since Don's handicap was now down to thirteen and he had to spend a lot more time at the course to make sure that it stayed there. I had gained a son but lost a husband.

At some point in her life every golf widow is likely to suffer from a case of the Sunday blues. Without exception the most depressing day in the golf widow's week is Sunday, the day God set aside for rest, for family sharing, for rejoicing. Sunday is the Sabbath, the holy day when the divine cycle of creation is commemorated.

> And on the seventh day God finished his work which he had done, and he rested on the seventh day from all his work which he had done. So God blessed the seventh day and hallowed it, because on it God rested from all his work which he had done in creation.
>
> Genesis 2:2–3

Thanks to our Judeo-Christian heritage, Sunday is, or used to be, the one day in the week that everyone could count on to rest from his or her weekly labours. The ritual restrictions that prohibit work on the Sabbath make it ideal for the central ritual in the avid golfer's life: Sunday is the

78

ideal day for the scheduling of golf tournaments. On Sundays most everyone has the leisure necessary to participate in golf tournaments. On any other day it is impossible to be certain of a good showing. Like God, the avid golfer has set aside Sunday and made it special. It is the one day during which he feels justly entitled to rest from his labours, and for the man who lives to golf there is only one pursuit suitable for the day. When a wife challenges a man's right to golf on the Sabbath, she attacks him in his holy of holies. She brings all he has worked for into question. Why is he slaving away to earn the money to feed, clothe, and shelter her and the kids if he is not permitted the one outing that makes the whole thing worthwhile? If he can't golf on Sundays, what's the point of it all?

The very same conditions that make Sunday ideal for golf make it depressing for the widow. Even if she is not a religious woman, she still suffers from her childhood associations of the sanctity of the Sabbath. "Remember the Sabbath day, to keep it holy" echoes in her brain. She knows that Sunday is the one day out of the week that she may not call up her friends and suggest an outing, realizing that their husbands will be home, that they will be enjoying a day of family rest and togetherness, and that any outside intrusion would be a profanation of the day. Hence the widow and her brood are left to their own devices. Sunday is different, and in communities like Chimo, where there is no Sunday shopping, Sundays can be a time when things that normally do not bother the widow take on new dimensions of gloom.

Sunday is the one day of the week when the head of the household could elect to stay at home. But where is the head? Where else? Every Sunday, unless it is raining or some other climatic disaster occurs, he elects to stay away. Each week the widow has to suffer the ignominy and humiliation of the knowledge that her husband would prefer to be out golfing with his buddies than in the company of his wife and family. He would rather be out chasing a little, white ball than in the bosom of his family.

Sunday is the day when the widow has the leisure to ponder the inequities of her situation. While her hubby is out having a good time with his buddies, she is left home alone to shoulder the load—the dirty diapers, the cat fights, the kid fights, the spilt milk. While she is left alone to cope with chicken pox, he goes off to Victoria for an intersquad with Rusty Oaks, arguing that he cannot let the team down. While she is busy washing his golf tees, ironing his scorecards, and polishing his balls, he is sipping a few cool ones in the lounge. While she is dusting off his trophies and scrubbing the green stains out of his pant cuffs, he is exchanging witticisms on the practice greens. While she is home with her head in the toilet, cleaning the bowl, he is out on the course planning which iron he should play next. It is at such moments that the widow knows that, while her husband's handicap is going down, hers is going up. While he is free to breeze out the door at 7:00 A.M. to return at 5:00 P.M. all fagged out from the day's play, she is left a virtual prisoner in her own home, outnumbered and outmaneuvered, two to one.

As she surveys her husband's sunburnt, slumbering form on the couch in front of the television, unkind thoughts start to formulate in her brain. As she observes his gaping mouth and listens to his full-volumed snores, she asks herself, "Is this where partnership leads?" And should he waken in a bitter mood and vent his spleen upon the widow's meal, she finds her thoughts are wont to turn sweetly to revenge.

Chapter 8
Golf Widow and Women's Lib

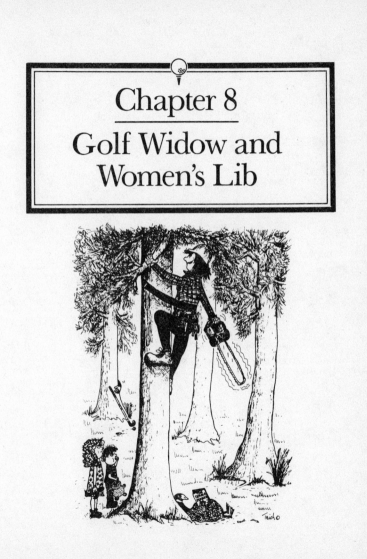

One sunny Sunday in May in the year of Our Lord, One Thousand Nine Hundred and Eighty-Three, as I was haunting the local schoolyard with my children at 7:00 A.M., I received a dramatic and sudden illumination. I was a single parent. The shock of this discovery left me momentarily dazed and bemused, and I did not see the return of the swing as it came back toward me. I was knocked down by the blow, but in response to my children's concerned cries I leapt quickly to my feet and prudently moved a few feet away from the swings. I was a single parent. Why had I not been able to see it before? In my bemused daze I tripped over the teeter-totter, sustaining a tear in my new beige slacks and a minor laceration to the knee. I arose and headed carefully in another direction. But I was a married woman. Wasn't there some sort of contradiction here? So thinking, I bumped my head inadvertently on the monkey bars and fell once more to my knees, ripping the knee out of the other pant leg. A slight cut had opened above my left eye, and a few drops of blood trickled into the pupil. I decided I had best stay where I was while pondering this deep, new insight into my situation.

To be more precise, the day was the second Sunday in May, the eighth day of May, or, in the special case of this year, the day was Mother's Day. To be fair I must admit that Don had gotten the children up and dressed, and the three of them had prepared my breakfast and brought it to me in bed. There I had enjoyed the meal along with the vista of dawn breaking in the east. It was 5:00 A.M. In order to accommodate the prescribed Mother's Day rituals, breakfast in bed had to be early so that Don could make his 6:56 A.M. tee time in the annual Mother's Day tournament. His handicap was now down to seven. His hand shook slightly as he poured my coffee, and I knew that his mind was on the day's play ahead. Low net was a prize that he had often won. His heart was now set on winning low gross. Breaking eighty had become old hat. Shooting par was now the big thrill, and shooting a subpar round was starting to become a definite possibility. Would today be the big day?

Thus it happened that on Mother's Day at approximately seven in the morning on the grounds of the Chimo Elementary School I learned my lesson. I had my epiphany. I was a single parent. Or, to be more precise, for the first time I acknowledged that I was a golf widow. I daubed the cut above my eye with my lace-trimmed handkerchief, assumed a pose reminiscent of Rodin's *Thinker*, and pursued this novel train of thought. For years I had avoided the truth of my situation. I had consoled myself with proverbial wisdom, thinking every couple is not a pair and knowing that everyone thinks her own burden the heaviest. I had long appreciated the fact that marrying is easy but housekeeping is hard, and I had known for many a year that *ye kenna* keep a man on land if his heart's at sea. But I was not wholly satisfied. I suffered from a vague discontent, knowing that for other women Sundays could be different.

I also suffered from the additional humiliation of knowing that I was a wimp. Thanks to the women's liberation movement, I had had my consciousness raised to the point where I knew that if Sundays were not all that I wished I should make them so. If I were a real woman, I would stand up for my rights and demand equal time on the course and in the home. I would demand that Don match me diaper for diaper, tea for tee, bottle for bottle, cup for cup, pin for pin, and apron for apron.

If I were a real woman, I would sign him up for a couples' workshop, insisting that there were a few problem areas in our relationship that we needed to iron out. Yet I never did, knowing full well what his response would be. He would ask which iron he should take, his six or his seven. Or would I want him to pack the steam iron? Chortle. Chortle. As far as Don was concerned, I was the one with the problem. And suddenly, I began to see that he just could be right.

What if it were the case that all along I had been deluding myself, pretending that Don was married to me and avoiding the truth that he was wedded to his golf? This error in my thinking would necessarily lead me to the wrong conclusions. However, if I were to revise my propositions, what would this do to the conclusions? What if I were to stop this little charade? If Don were married to his golf game, then it would be only right and proper that he should spend his Sundays with her, fondling his clubs in search of the holes in her close-shaven greens. Of course he would be better off with better balls. Why hadn't I been able to appreciate this before?

Instead of wallowing in self-pity, I would start operating on different assumptions. Instead of resenting Don's golf, I would learn to recognize it for what it was. Having rid myself of the last of my illusions, I could get on with the job of rearing the children and running the household with a clear sense of purpose and a new sense of pride. I would ask myself, "What would the single parent do in this situation?" and give myself back the self-evident answer: "She would do it herself."

Since May 8, 1983, I have become a changed woman, a woman proud of her accomplishments. Instead of wasting time thinking that Don ought to be around more of the time, taking a greater interest in his children and their upbringing, or even spending more time with his wife, I have come to cherish my newly conceived independence. I had long appreciated that Don did not wish to be troubled by domestic trivia that might throw him off his game. I could understand that chopping wood was bad since it could lead to calluses and blisters on his hand that would destroy his putting touch. I knew that expecting him to change a tire was also out of the question since he might wrench his arm while pumping the jack and throw off his swing for weeks. I could appreciate that if I were left in charge of things at home he would be free to develop the mental concentration necessary to keep his handicap going in the right direction. Consequently, I had become quite handy about the house after years of doing the little odd jobs that have habitually been the province of the male. Now, I realized, I should take pride in these accomplishments.

After all, any woman who could start off unable to grasp the mechanics involved in changing a light bulb at the commencement of her married life and find herself fourteen years later able to change the ballast in her fluorescent lights should be proud of herself. Any woman able to plan the rewiring for an addition to the house that she had designed and would soon commence construction on must needs be, in a very significant sense, liberated. Any woman who could go from a total lack of appreciation of car maintenance to giving her 1966 Chevrolet Bel-Air a lube and oil and a tune-up must be well on her way to reliance on self. Any woman who could rotate the tires on her car by simply lifting up the rear end with her right hand and then bending over to yank off the hubcap with her left and loosen the bolts with her teeth should, justifiably, think that Wonder Woman had better tighten her lasso.

I perceived that Sundays could be different. I could hire a regular baby-sitter and do whatever I pleased. I figured out that what was good enough for God and the avid golfer was good enough for me. Now we are all free to rest from our regular activities and do whatever it is that pleases us most.

Best of all, I stopped taking Don's golf as a personal affront. I became detached from it in the finest scientific spirit and began to gain new insights into the behaviour of the golfer that before had been obscured by my own prejudices and false expectations. I began to see the thing in its true light.

Now when I strap on my tool belt and reach down for my chainsaw and hard hat on my way out to the back of our property to cut down a few Douglas firs for the wood for the addition, I have a new sense of pride in my abilities. These are skills I would not have acquired had it not been for Don's golf. Not only can I sew and reap, cook and clean; I can also build and weld. Now when I slip on my lumberjack boots with the steel toes, put on my spurs, and run up a tree, I no longer feel that something is amiss, that I am not the one who ought to be doing this. Now I am more inclined to shout, "Germaine Greer, look out! Particularly if you are standing 'neath this tree."

Chapter 9

Hole-in-One *or* The Numerology of Golf

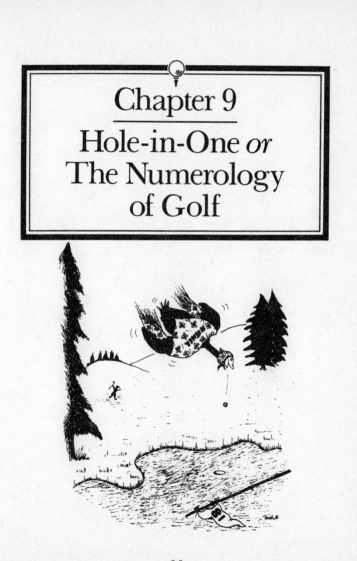

In theory at least, it is always possible for a man to improve his golf game, to reduce the number of strokes that it takes him to play a round. Every man who comes off the course can cite at least five instances when his score should have been lower. Had it not been for the rub of the green, a loose impediment, or another sort of dropping left by one of the expletive-deleted geese, he could have knocked four strokes off his score. If he had not been distracted by a low-flying helicopter, a sudden movement by someone in his foursome, or an unexpected chortle that caused him to lose his concentration and muff his drive, he would have shot his best round ever. By the time a man has come off the course and arrived at the pro shop he knows that his score is not what it should have been.

"I shot ninety-one, but with any luck at all it

should have been an eighty-five. I was only five feet from the pin on eight, and I three-putted! On my first putt my ball hit a spike mark and veered three feet to the right and ended up ten feet from the pin. I couldn't believe it! I three-putted when I should have had an easy birdie. They shouldn't allow all these bush league tournaments on the course. All they do is tear up the greens for the members.''

Ask any man who has just come off the course what he shot, and he will tell you that he shot an eighty-nine but should have shot an eighty, and would have, if it hadn't been for the expletive-deleted . . .

Ask another one who has just come off the course, and he will tell you that he shot an eighty-five but should have shot a seventy-eight, and would have, if it hadn't been for the expletive-deleted . . .

Usually you don't need to ask a golfer what he shot and what he should have shot. He will tell you straight out. However, I have yet to hear a golfer come off the course and say:

"I shot a ninety-two, and I was darn lucky to get that. If it hadn't been for that spike mark on eight, I would have missed the hole by five feet. By gad, I was lucky my ball hit that spike mark, or I could have taken another three strokes to get back up to the pin. The way they've got the pin placed today, if you miss your putt low, you'll roll down the slope, all the way to the fringe. Thanks to that spike mark, I salvaged par.

"Then, on thirteen, I was going out of bounds for sure, and if my ball hadn't hit the side of that low-flying helicopter and careened back onto the green, I would have had another two strokes for going OB. As it was I made birdie.

"But that was nothing. You won't believe how lucky I got at eighteen. As usual, I muffed my drive. I don't know why, but I always skull the ball at eighteen. Then I really shanked my second shot. It was certain to land in the water hazard, and would have, too, if it hadn't have been for the old mother goose. I guess she was afraid my ball was going to hit one of her goslings. Anyway, what does the old bird do? She opens her beak and catches the ball as neat as you please. Then the old girl flaps her wings, runs a few steps on the water, and takes off. With my ball! My best Hogan! But be damned if she doesn't head straight for the pin, circle it twice, and drop my ball right in the hole. I couldn't believe it. If she hadn't done that, God knows how many extra shots I would have had. As it was, I got an eagle! My first. An eagle on eighteen, thanks to a goose!"

Theoretically, it is always possible for a man to

improve his golf game. Not only can he think of numerous instances during each round when he should have made a better score, but if he could just improve each game, he could lower his handicap. Then when he was asked, "What's your handicap?" he could say, "Twelve." Period. He would not have to explain that this week it had just been raised to fifteen but that he's really a twelve, and would be still, if it weren't for the expletive-deleted . . .

The simple truth is that all golfers have vivid imaginations when it comes to the accuracy of their scores. Ask any golfer, and he will tell you that his score is not what it should have been. And every club has its sandbagger, the man who will pad his handicap so that he may win all the tournaments. However, it is not my intention here to dwell on the seamier side of the numbers game. I merely mention it in passing. I merely scratch the surface. My concern is with the mystical side of the numbers game, the numerology of golf.

The numerology of golf is a topic few have commented on, and it might have escaped even my notice, had it not been for Don's hole-in-one. Had it not been for Don's ace, I might have missed one of the central features of the game of golf—its ability to enrapture, or the spellbinding dimension of the game. In short, I might have missed the magic.

June 22, 1983, began in the ordinary way. The sun dragged itself above the craggy peaks of the coast range, took a deep breath, and freed itself from their clutches. Then it cast its bored sunbeams on the lackadaisical waters of the strait and sauntered up the sky, erasing the prosaic purple mists of the dawn on its habitual path to the noon zenith. My Don was already on his habitual path to the club for breakfast with his buddies before they set out for their daily round of golf. As usual, I was up making breakfast for the children, getting the beds made, the wash in, the vacuuming done, the wood chopped, the garden watered, the flowerbeds weeded, and the lawn mowed before the semi from the mill arrived to pick up the Douglas fir logs for the addition. There was nothing to indicate that this summer day was to be different from any other summer day.

Don ordered his usual breakfast of crisp bacon, one fried egg over easy, two slices of brown toast with strawberry jam, apple juice, and hot chocolate. I cannot remember his telling me what his buddies ordered. After breakfast the habitually jovial foursome got their golf bags out of storage at the pro shop. In unison they took out their putters and commenced practicing their bad shots on the practice green, exchanging witticisms all the while. Then, as if by some prearranged signal, their expressions sobered scientifically. They put away their putters and started down the path to the first tee, for at 6:56 A.M., as usual, they were due off.

To be honest, I have to admit that I cannot remember what Don told me he made on the first three holes. I think it was bogey, bogey, par. But it could have been par, bogey, bogey, or even, par, bogey, birdie. I know it wasn't birdie, birdie, birdie, although it might have been par, birdie, par, or even double bogey, par, birdie. Don sometimes has a little trouble with the first hole, which is a par five, despite the fact that he usually booms his drives. Either he gets a bad case of the hooks, which puts him on the practice tee, or he slices his ball into the woods on the right. In any case, it really doesn't matter what Don scored on one, two, or three because the big moment took place on four.

I really can't do justice to the event, for I have trouble recalling what the fourth hole at the Chimo Club looks like, although I have been there many times. I'm pretty sure it's a par three, and I'm pretty sure it's the hole I'm happiest to see after my usual disastrous starts. I think Don used a seven iron. On the other hand, it must have been his eight. The men he plays with talk a lot about Don's great eight-iron shots. When Don uses his eight, most of his regular playing partners are using a six, and some of them even have to use a wood. I'm pretty sure it was his eight iron. Anyway, on that day, June 22, 1983, which had begun so much like any other day, Don teed up and got a hole-in-one on the fourth hole.

Don aced the fourth hole and went into orbit for a week. At the end of the week his joy was somewhat mitigated by the fact that a female member of the club, one of the does, got a hole-in-one, albeit on eight, a much shorter par three. However, the rapturous delight, the sheer transport the event caused was a marvel to behold.

Most golfers never experience the thrill of making a hole-in-one. Indeed, many of the priests go to their graves without making one. Thus it would seem that getting a hole-in-one is more a matter of chance than of skill. Therefore, every time a man tees up at a par three, or even the occasional par four, the possibility of acing it is there, and each man is likely to ask himself if today might be the day.

At the Chimo Club, whenever a man or a

woman makes a hole-in-one, there are free drinks on the house to celebrate the event. In this manner all of the members who happen to be present at the time get a chance to share in the wonder of the moment. They get a chance to share in the high. However, some manage to get quite a bit higher than others. Then, as a permanent tribute, Chimo Securities and Finance Ltd. presents the lucky man or woman with a trophy depicting a one with a hole in it and a face plate on the base giving the member's name, the date, and the hole at which the wonder occurred.

I think it was the sight of the trophy, the physical object itself, that started my musings on the numerology of golf. The sight of the zero in the one and the perception of the depth of Don's joy together started me thinking that there might be more to this golfing business than meets the eye. Perhaps the simple brainwashing theory was too obvious. Perhaps there were some unseen forces at work here. Perhaps there was some magic.

Don is a six. When I assert this, I do not mean that he plays golf to a six handicap, that he normally completes a round of golf by taking six strokes more than par. When I say Don is a six, I mean that Don's number of destiny is six. I mean that when you add up the numbers in the date of Don's birth numerologically, you will end up with six, or his number of destiny.

Don was born on·July 8, 1944. Adding these numbers up according to the time-honoured principles of numerology, one gets the following sum:

$$
\begin{array}{r}
1944 \\
7 \\
+ \quad 8 \\
\hline
1959
\end{array}
$$

Next, one must add up the numbers in the total thus arrived at:

$$1 + 9 + 5 + 9 = 24$$

Similarly,

$$2 + 4 = 6$$

Therefore, six is Don's number of destiny.

The date on which Don's hole-in-one occurred was June 22, 1983. June is the *sixth* month in the year. Twenty-two is a master power number. Thus, numerology teaches us, we should not be surprised when Don, a six, gets a hole-in-one in the sixth month of a year, particularly on a day with a master power number. That it should occur on the fourth hole is also easily comprehensible when one remembers that our six was born in 1944. Note the doubled fours. Note also that nine is the number of power and completion and that one is the number that a golfer marks down on his card when he makes a hole-in-one. When we also note that two plus two equals four and that the iron used to make the shot was an eight-iron, a number divisible by four, the whole mystery is cleared up. The thing becomes self-evident. Don was born on the *eighth* day of the month.

As I pondered the numerical subtleties of Don's hole-in-one I began to see that this type of analysis could have a much wider application. I began to see that numerology is woven into the very fabric of the game. I perceived that those old shepherds were more than perverse. They were tricky and crazy as well. To support this thesis I need only cite the example of the Old Course at Saint Andrews, which is appropriately laid out in the shape of a shepherd's crook. On the Old Course, seven of the greens are doubled. To the untrained eye this unique feature of the course is simply part of the quaint, Old World charm of the

links. It is merely one of the many features that make Saint Andrews so special. When visitors are informed that the numbers of the holes that share the doubled greens add up to eighteen, they are apt to exclaim, "How quaint!" or "How clever!" For indeed, any schoolboy knows that:

$$2 + 16 = 18$$
$$3 + 15 = 18$$
$$4 + 14 = 18$$
$$5 + 13 = 18$$
$$6 + 12 = 18$$
$$7 + 11 = 18$$

and that:

$$8 + 10 = 18.$$

This is pure numerology, which, in its elementary phases, is accessible to all who can add. However, what the average schoolboy will not know is that two is the number of irrationality and trickery. The trained numerologist, on the other hand, knows that two stands for duplicity. Therefore, as soon as a numerologist hits a doubled green, his or her senses are piqued and he or she suspects that something fishy is likely to happen, particularly on a course situated on the Firth of Tay at the estuary of the Eden River.

Two is the number of trickery, magic, and

duplicity. It is the number of destiny most often associated with crooks, be they shepherds' or not. Two is intimately connected with golf. However, the number inseparably conjoined to the game is nine. Golf is traditionally played on courses consisting of eighteen holes divided into two halves, the front nine and the back nine. On Royal and Ancient courses the ninth hole is usually the farthest hole from the clubhouse so a golfer must play the home nine to avoid losing face. As the game has evolved in North America, the ninth and the eighteenth holes are usually situated in such a way as to facilitate easy access to the clubhouse. Following the same principles that have exalted the institution of Stag Night in North America, the golf course architects on this side of the water have designed the courses in such a way so that a man can always, conveniently and inconspicuously, get back his nerve. Thus, if a man's nerve fails him after the front nine, he can make a quick trip to the lounge before starting off again on ten. Or he can call it quits and remain in the lounge for the rest of the day.

In addition to being the number of power and completion, nine is the number of elimination. It is unique amongst the nine digits in that it is the only number that, when added to any other number, disappears or eliminates itself. For example, seven plus five equals twelve. When twelve is reduced to its numerological base by adding the one and the two, the sum obtained is three—a number distinct from either the seven or the five. However, when nine is the addend, the number to which it is added remains as the numerological base. For example, seven plus nine equals sixteen, and one plus six equals seven. The seven remains. If one and nine are added together we get the sum of ten. One plus zero is one, and we find ourselves back where we started. The nine always eliminates itself, except on the golf course, where nine is always added to nine and, therefore, cannot disappear as it is wont to do. Like the avid golfer, it keeps coming back.

Nine is also the number associated with Neptune, an ancient Roman god of fresh water, who was later identified with Poseidon and subsequently became famous as a sea god, a god of the deep, a god conversant with tides and the moon. Neptune is the name given to the planet whose discovery was necessitated to account for calculations whose accuracy could be justified only if there were a planet out there exerting sufficient gravitational pull. In fact, it was the complexity of the calculations of gravitational effects that led

to the invention of the computer. The computer was not invented, as is widely believed in some circles, to facilitate the job of the nine-man USGA

Handicap Research Team, intricate as their computations may be. Equally wrong-headed are those who question why the USGA would pick nine men for the job and not six or eight or even twelve. Once the numerological principles of golf are understood, nine is seen to be the only possible choice.

Once we understand that the inventors of the game of golf were directly influenced from the beginning by numerology, Neptune, and the ebb and flow of tides, by the waxing and waning of the moon, by its gravitational pull, the lunatic lengths that some will go to in pursuit of a little, white ball start to make sense. For what is gravity if it is not an unseen force whose strength and effects are calculated numerically? And what is magic but an unseen force? Hence all those golfers who play with their numbers should beware of the forces they might unwittingly effect.

Finally, when some describe the Old Course as a moonscape or a lunar surface, we should not be surprised. Similarly, when the Americans successfully land an eagle on the moon, is it any wonder that a Shepard should get out and hit two shots with a six-iron? After all, two is the number of trickery. A six is an upside-down nine. And the moon, when full, is a little, white ball.

Chapter 10
Winter Vacation

olfers, like geese, prefer to go south for the winter. They like to winter in the sun, where the living is easy and the golfing is good. Each fall, when the maple leaves start to turn crimson and gold and the wind blows clear and cold from the north, the members of the Chimo Club start to grow restless and chippy. They can be seen in the lounge pacing up and down the room in a state of agitation uncommon at any other time of the year. They huddle together in little V-shaped flocks, discussing flight patterns and accommodation arrangements.

Some golfers, who still feel a touch of sentiment and the pull of familial ties, elect to spend the Christmas season at home. Others, like Don, who cannot arrange a winter vacation are forced to stay home. To cater to the needs of these poor souls the

Chimo Club organizes a couple of tournaments—the one held on Boxing Day and the one held on New Year's Day. However, these events are often rained out, and, given the paucity of the membership at this time of the year, they usually draw a small group of devotees at best. By the New Year every golfer worth his salt has gone south. Consequently, there is an empty and desolate air at the club in the winter, except in the ballroom, where the card tables remain permanently set up for the bridge fanatics, and except in the dining room, which now opens its doors to nonmembers for lunch and dinner.

It is during the winter that Don finds himself most disadvantaged in his choice of career. Unlike the mill worker, the retired member, the professional, or the self-employed businessman, the academic is tied to the timetable set by the school year. Going south with the geese is not possible, unless the academic is on leave or on sabbatical. However, since going on leave means getting no pay, and going on sabbatical is possible only once every seven years, Don was becoming the habitual double winner of the Boxing Day and New Year's Day tournaments. But the victories were small compensation for his having to stay home and share the club with the bridge players and the dinner crowd. He longed to be with his buddies down south. Finally, his sabbatical turn came, and for the first time since his arrival in Chimo, a winter vacation became a beatific reality.

The wintering hole most favoured by Chimo Club golfers is that part of the planet in and around Palm Springs, California. Palm Springs is the avid golfer's Mecca. The native Californian, on the other hand, knows that Mecca is a little community about thirty miles southeast of Palm Springs on the road to the Salton Sea. Thanks to the vast underground river that courses under the desert valley floor, the arid landscape has become a manmade golfing paradise. Here there are more golf courses per square foot than in any other place on earth. Palm Springs and the surrounding territory is the second holiest shrine next to Saint Andrews on the avid golfer's map. It is the place of his annual winter pilgrimage, and it was Don's choice for our first winter vacation.

Given the large number of pilgrims from western Canada who fly south in the winter, it is possible to get a direct flight from Vancouver to Palm Springs. While Don busied himself making the travel arrangements for his golfing equipment, I busied myself making the travel arrangements for everyone and everything else—a considerable task since we had decided to take the children, and our son was still a colicky five-month-old baby. While Don carefully packed his clubs, his balls, his tees, his golfing shoes, and his golf bag into the travel bag that he had borrowed, I packed our swimming suits, sun hats, and suntan lotion; our tickets, traveller's cheques, and Visa card; the Snuggli, the stroller, and the diaper bag. I think I was able to squeeze it all into four suitcases. As Don beat a path to the check-in counter at the airport and gave the agents detailed instructions for the safe transport of his clubs, I brought up the rear with the baby in the Snuggli on my chest, the suitcases strapped to the stroller, and our daughter and the diaper bag securely gripped in my one free hand. Two hours later we were in the Palm Springs airport.

Once we were settled into a spacious housekeeping unit in one of the local motels, I began to see that a vacation with a golfer is much like being at home for a two-week period in which each day feels like Sunday. Life with two children does not change much no matter where you are, although I did have the additional excitement of trying to keep my nonswimmer out of the deep end of the pool. We soon settled into a daily routine. Don would get up at daybreak. He would then waken three of his buddies from Chimo, who happened to be staying at the same motel, and then the four of them would go out for breakfast before they began scouting for a course on which to play. I, too, would be up at dawn, and, after getting the children fed and clothed, we would begin our daily trek in search of food. While Don was out hunting, I was out gathering, and life assumed a primitive pace.

For Chimo golfers the winter pilgrimage culminates with the celebration of the major religious festival in the avid golfer's year—the Bob Hope Desert Classic. Don was no exception to this rule, and the four days that he spent at the Classic remain amongst the fondest memories of his life. Someday, in later years, he would really have something to tell his grandchildren: he had seen some of the highest priests in person. I could not boast the same, for, being a stranger in town, I did not know a reliable baby-sitter. However, I did manage to watch some of the show on television.

According to the ABC commentators for the event, the Desert Classic is the most-watched golf tournament in America today. The unique feature of the Classic, a feature much copied of late, is that it permits the men who live to golf onto the course with the men who golf to live. It is one of the few times when the ordinary golfer may enter the sacred cycle of the Gold Trail tournaments and play around with the priests. The only stipulation is that the ordinary golfer must have plenty of gold. A few friends on the tournament's organizing committee don't hurt either.

Playing in the Classic is the highest blessing the rich, ordinary golfer may obtain. Like the sale of the infamous indulgences of old, heaven is for those who can buy their way in, for appearing in this tournament is akin to achieving a state of grace. By allowing ordinary mortals into the tournament, the event celebrates the American Dream—that anyone who earns money the old-fashioned way will be rewarded. Each year the Bob Hope Desert Classic reaffirms the fact that in America the rich are blessed. They may golf with the priests and hobnob with the stars.

That golf is an affliction that knows no social bounds is evidenced by the number of celebrities who unabashedly step in front of television cameras and let their swings be shown uncensored. Hollywood stars, like the aristocrats of yore, are becoming golf enthusiasts. Despite the best advice of their agents, these celebrities are willing to let us see their clay feet. For all these spellbound souls, stepping onto the first tee marks the definitive moment in their lives beside which birth, death, money, power, fame, war, and sex are trifles of no concern. They have embarked upon a quest for the mastery of the game of golf from which there is no return voyage. In awe of the majesty and dimension of the game, they are humble and fall down in worship at the feet of that holy and elusive grail called *golf*. Forever and ever. Amen.

For the nongolfer—those still concerned with birth, death, money, power, fame, war, and sex— Palm Springs has much to offer. It boasts as many movie stars, past and present, as Beverly Hills; and, unlike Beverly Hills, it is still possible to take a celebrity tour. For the nongolfer likes to make pilgrimages, too. And for those stuck in Palm Springs without a car, the tour bus will pick you up at the door of your motel, or in the lobby of the Hilton, as the case may be. They will even let you bring the children.

Here in the land where mailboxes have piano keys, where authentic Grecian statues grace private gardens, where interior decoration runs the gamut of Contemporary Mediterranean through Exotic Contemporary, with delightful overtones of the dramatic Orient, to just plain Contemporary with dashes of Louis Quinze—here, where the bedspreads will shock you, the colour scheme startle you, the vistas surprise you, the carved doors amaze you, and the prices astound you, you are encouraged to stroll at your leisure and contemplate the fountains, the carpets, the pianos, the shutters, the bathrooms, or the pools. You are permitted to sit down by the bougainvillea under a palm tree and enjoy a succulent date milkshake followed by a chaser of Von's freshly squeezed orange juice, provided you remember to place the disposable goblets in the gold leaf garbage cans.

Palm Springs is the Big Time. Here the Beautiful People are wont to gather. Here the streets buzz with the news that Liz is in town, that Liza and Shirley are dining at Alberto's, that Frank's electronic surveillance system is back up so he must be home, that Lucy has a cold, that Bob was seen walking down Palm Canyon Drive in 1957, and that Spencer Tracy's ghost was just spotted in the Cornelia White House. Here the locals drive Rolls Royce and Mercedes-Benz golf carts. Here there are temples and temples, and pools where Shirley Temple played as a child.

Nonetheless, life at the top is not without its trauma. The problem with earthly paradises is that the treasure cannot be stored up in heaven; it must be locked up down here on earth. The problem with gold is that it glitters and can be seen for miles. The lasting impression that one takes home from Palm Springs is that the place must be filled with crooks, be they shepherds' or not. For how else can one explain the plethora of security systems, fences, alarms, dogs, guards, cars, gates, and weapons that fortify the town? There is a peculiar irony about so much security: it makes one feel insecure. But only for a moment. For here there are too many delights to engage the senses. Here in this twentieth-century Shangri-la, all of the material elements that epitomize heaven on earth may be savoured, provided one has enough gold and an automobile, preferably chauffeur-driven, for the city's unwritten motto reads: "Never let it be said that there is anything pedestrian about Palm Springs."

As our plane climbed high above the desert valley floor and we watched the last rays of the sun sink below the peak of Mount San Jacinto, I reflected that the trip had been worth it, particularly when I contemplated the sleeping, suntanned faces of the children. However, I resolved, the next time Don could go alone, like the rest of his buddies. As the sun set, we all settled back in our seats, innocent of the fact that, while we were headed for Vancouver and a snowstorm, our luggage was en route to Calgary; that is, except for Don's golf clubs, which, thanks to Don's last-minute arrival at the airport and his special instruction, arrived at the correct destination.

Chapter 11
Club Captain

In the fall of 1982 Don was elected captain of the Chimo Golf and Country Club. Dramatic as the event seemed at the time, the way for his meteoric rise to the top had been paved by his earlier decision that he had a responsibility to the club above and beyond the straightforward payment of his dues. As early as 1980 he had begun to feel that it was time that he gave something back to the game that had given him so much.

Don began modestly enough, helping out some of the dedicated souls on the Match and Handicap Committee with the purchase of prizes awarded to the winners at the Chimo Club tournaments. This is a little-publicized but time-consuming job given the plenteous number of prizes given out at every tournament and given the plenteous number of tournaments held. During the summer there may be an average of one tournament per Sunday.

During a really good summer there will be an average of two tournaments per Sunday. Each Sunday during the summer, after the entrants have finished their rounds and all the scores are in, the stags gather in the banquet hall for moose steak, moose juice, and the afternoon's entertainment.

The first prize that is customarily handed out amid heartfelt and admiring applause is the coveted prize for overall low gross. This prize is not awarded for the dirtiest joke of the day; rather, it is given to the man who has completed his round and taken the fewest strokes at his ball. The second prize awarded is usually for overall low net, which is given to the man with the lowest score after the subtraction of his handicap, be it one or thirty-one, from the number of strokes that he took at his ball. The man who has the lowest net score is given second pick of the loot. However, whether or not overall low net is truly the second most prestigious prize of the day seems to be a moot point given that this stag is usually treated to a thunderous ovation of cheers, jeers, and chants of "Porchie, Porchie, Porchie."

After the uproar subsides, the entertainment continues, for there are prizes for low gross, low net, second low gross, and second low net in each flight or handicap division—for flights A, B, C, D,

126

E, F, G, H, I, and M and S, if necessary. In addition, the Match and Handicap Committee might decide to award prizes for the longest putt on seventeen, the shortest drive on two, or KP (closest to the pin) on fourteen. Sometimes there are even free balls for all. The principle here seems to be that, like birthday parties, it is important to send as many of the participants home as happy as possible. No one should feel left out.

The position of club captain is an awkward one, as Don quickly learned. Historically, the position has been a prestigious one—an honour given to the man whose play on the course has been inspiring and whose conduct has been exemplary. The grounds for selection are thus comparable to those used for the selection of the captain of a hockey team. The club captain is supervisor of play on the course. It is his job to make rulings at the tournaments, set the members' handicaps, and expel players, if need be, for bad language, dangerous play, or offensive behaviour in the clubhouse. Therefore, in practice, the job can prove hazardous to the captain's health. The only redeeming part of the job is that it comes with a reserved parking spot right by the pro shop, for unlike the captain of a hockey team, the club captain does not even get a big *C* to sew on his sweater.

The club captain is also responsible for doing all the draws for the tournaments; at least he is at the Chimo Club. Consequently, the captain must remain close to Chimo for the entire term of his captaincy. At times, this may be a bitter pill to swallow, for another one of the perks that comes with the job is that the club captain is given honourary memberships in brother establishments. He is even liable to receive red velvet-embossed invitations to join His Royal Highness, the Prince, and the Lucifer Society in a little tournament at the Royal Lytham St. Anne's. The catch-22 is that the club captain is too busy at home to take advantage of royal invitations. He doesn't even have the time to play a round at Rusty Oaks.

At the same time that Don became club captain he was also elected to the position of director, there being nothing in the bylaws to suggest that service to the club in the dual capacity of captain and director might be considered to fall within the category of conflict of interest. Had I been consulted, I could have helped put the record straight. Had I been able to get my hands on the two-timing so-and-so, I could have shown him a thing or two about conflict of interest. But I was never asked, and I never saw Don long enough to voice a protest, for he was now rarely ever home.

Club Captain

During the winter Don was still teaching night courses so that he could get in his daily round of golf. This was nothing new. But now, during the summer, he was never home either, not even at night. If he wasn't at Stag Night, he was doing the draw for the upcoming tournament. If he wasn't doing the draw for the upcoming tournament, he was at a director's meeting. If he wasn't at a director's meeting, he was at a regular meeting. If he wasn't at a regular meeting, he was at an irregular meeting. If he wasn't at an irregular meeting, he was at a breakfast meeting. If he wasn't at a breakfast meeting, he was at a luncheon meeting. Small wonder that he and I could not come to a meeting of the minds. For if Don was not meeting, he was sleeping, and I had started leaving his dinner out on the front porch beside the cats'.

I was a single parent. True enough. But I had none of the advantages that being on one's own can bring. I was tied to the house just in case Don might make one of his infrequent pit stops. I had to be ready, on a moment's notice, to change his oil, fill his tank, rotate his tires, and push him back out on the track. I was also kept extremely busy answering the telephone, fielding all the messages from irate golfers trying to contact Don. "If you see him," I'd say encouragingly, "take a swing at him for me, will you?" Consequently, I gained an insight into the machinations at the club that a widow is not normally privy to.

As I soon learned, golf club politics are no laughing matter. They are a subject not open to jest. The issues debated inside the cloistered confines of the club by the members and their directors have a purity that the tawdry affairs of everyday life lack. In particular, the directors themselves, having undertaken their roles in a spirit of *noblesse oblige*, volunteering their time for the benefit of the common *weal*, thereby obtain a position of moral superiority that ordinary mortals cannot pretend to.

In contrast to the worldwide problems of international disarmament, nuclear holocaust, technological revolution, acid rain, the greenhouse effect, and Third World poverty, the issues debated at the club—what colour to paint the lounge walls, what sort of chairs to purchase, whether or not to enlarge the men's changing rooms and hire a masseuse, whether or not to serve hot lunches to the general public—are all issues a man can really sink his teeth into. Here debate is honed down to a simple purity. The issues are local and fall within the sphere of possible action.

"Do we need to redecorate and enlarge the men's changing rooms?"

"Can we afford it?"

"If we do decide to do it, how much should we spend?"

"Should we hire an interior decorator?"

"If we do hire an interior decorator, who should it be?"

"How much should we pay aforementioned, hypothetical interior decorator in the possible event that we decide to hire one?"

"How much should the aforementioned, hypothetical interior decorator be allowed to spend, in the possible event that we decide to hire one?"

"Should the interior decorator be given *carte blanche*, up to a certain amount, agreed upon beforehand that is acceptable to the membership?"

"Can we afford it?"

"Do we need to redecorate and enlarge the men's changing rooms?"

These are seemingly simple problems with simple solutions that should be obvious, even to a director. Yet it is simple issues such as these that can become the catalyst for violent debate and the wholesale resignation of boards and boards of directors.

What seems to me to be really at stake here is the participants' honour and integrity; to wit, a man's reputation. Consequently, political affairs at the club can erupt with a suddenness that the membership at large may find astonishing. They may go to bed one night confident that the club political machinery is humming along without a squeak, only to awaken the next morning to learn that the board has resigned *en masse* and there are various splinter groups now at loggerheads in the clubhouse. Perhaps this is just another way of getting rid of the deadwood. Since the time-honoured solution of dueling pistols at dawn has receded into the mists of time, there can be no clear winner in these affairs of the heart. Social relations can become strained. Manners may take second place to the issues at hand. Some of the phone calls may have to be prefaced with a discreet query.

"Are you at liberty to speak freely? Nod once for yes. Twice for no."

Some of the splinters may start lurking in dark corners of the lounge, forming little knothole gangs, plotting their next move.

"Psssst. I'd like to speak to you about you-know-who and you-know-what."

"You mean . . ."

"Shhh. Not here! Lower your voice. We've got a little splinter group over in the corner where we can talk more freely. All we need is enough proxies, and we might have enough for a knothole

132

gang. If we can form a gang, we might have enough green wood for a new board. At the very least we can make a plank and build a platform."

I have seen perfectly respectable businessmen, neatly attired in club blazer, white shirt, and school tie, become so preoccupied with political affairs at the club that they forget common courtesy altogether. They are likely to come sneaking up to an ex-director's table, their necks turning in a 360-degree radius to ensure that the coast is clear, lean over their victim's ear, and whisper loudly, "Pssst. I'd like to speak to you about you-know-who and you-know-what." Many drinks are spilled in surprise at such approach shots.

However, spilled drinks are the least of the Chimo Club golfer's concerns. For the past four or five years now the most chronic problem at the club has been the Canada geese who have made their permanent home on the pastoral environs of the fairways, the greens, and the water hazards. For some reason these geese have lost their homing instinct and remain in permanent settlement on the course. What has caused these geese to resist the migrational pull of centuries of genetic coding has baffled the best minds at the Chimo Biological Station. My own hypothesis is that either the geese have had this aberrant behaviour imprinted on them as goslings by their mistaken imitation of the golfers' example, or that this abnormality is caused by some unknown virus and the entire club is infected. The whole membership has lost its homing instinct, and this infection has spread to the geese.

Geese have a number of endearing characteristics. Unlike ducks, in geese the sexes are alike in size, plumage, and markings. At a glance it is impossible to tell the gander from the goose. Also, the males assist the females in the upbringing of the young. However, it is not this characteristic that the golfers at the Chimo Club object to. They object to the little droppings of excrement these birds are continually spreading over the course. Golfers unaccustomed to the art of the diaper change are liable to get particularly distressed by this rude invasion of Nature into their manicured domain.

In fact, the droppings of a forty-pound goose are not so little. They can be quite considerable. Goose shit interferes with play on the course. Any ball that has landed in a nice warm dropping is liable to take unusual dips in its subsequent trajectories. Since golfers are not allowed to clean their balls between tee and green, this can have serious consequences for a golfer's score. Goose shit can make the short game impossible or a putt unsinkable.

Each year the size of the flock had gotten a little bit larger, and the problem was obvious to all of the members. The matter had been raised at a number of meetings of the board, but it had always been pushed aside by the burning issue of the moment. Every once in a while someone would shout out a complaint from the floor, but

these shouts were ignored by board after board.

"When are you going to do something about the goose shit?"

"Don't you think it's time that somebody did something about the geese? I ruined two pairs of golf shoes in one week. I think the membership has a right to some kind of compensation."

"If someone doesn't do something about the geese soon, someone could get hurt. Those birds are starting to turn vicious. Since the death of their leader yesterday there have been three cases of geese attacks. Someone's going to get their eyes pecked out. If you guys don't do something soon, I'm going to go out there with my twenty-two and turn the whole lot into goose stew."

"When is someone going to do something about the poachers on the course? The guys are getting so bold that they're dragging the geese off in broad daylight. And ruining my short game. How is a man supposed to concentrate?"

"What are you going to do about all the corpses? How many geese have to die from golf ball wounds before you people will take some action? If you don't do something soon, I'm going to call the SPCA."

"What do you mean the SPCA doesn't investigate bird calls?"

"When are you guys going to do something about the goose shit?"

"When are the captains going to big *C*'s for their sweaters?"

"If we don't do something about these geese soon, we could all do hard time for hunting without a license out of season. It's only a matter of time before the Fish and Wildlife boys get called in by an irate member. And those guys carry guns!"

"This whole issue is going to blow up in our faces. The environmentalists might move in. Green Peace might stage a sit-in and occupy the clubhouse. The next thing you know the press will be here, snapping pictures and running editorials. The reputation of the club will be dragged through the mud."

It was becoming obvious to the directors that they were now forced to take action. They called a special meeting for dealing with extraordinary business under *Robert's Rules of Order*, Article V, Section 36, Paragraph 4. After lengthy debate it was moved, seconded, and unanimously passed that nothing should be done about the geese, for the obvious reason that, given the law of averages, one of the birds was bound to start laying golden eggs soon. Further, it was moved, seconded, and passed unanimously that, for the purposes of safeguarding the interests of the club, the members, and the geese, a little goose girl would be hired to shepherd the flock. The very next day the does, who had been extremely skittish of late, got wind of this decision. As soon as the scent filtered through the herd, they stampeded through the new addition to the men's changing rooms and demolished the whole thing. The current board is in hiding, and until they reappear, nothing may be done. Meanwhile the geese remain on the course.

Chapter 12
Revenge, at Last

Every man can guide an ill wife but him that has her.

American Proverb

It is a maxim of mortal life that most men marry, that fire in the heart sends smoke into the brain. Golfers are no exception to this rule. Most golfers have wives. However, during the twelve years that Don has been a member of the Chimo Golf and Country Club I have come to see that most golfers do not like to admit to having a wife. They like to pretend that they are free to play a round whenever they wish. This gives the dynamics of a golfer's marital relations a special edge. In the sanctuary of the club the golfer seeks asylum from the trials and tribulations of married life. While in the clubhouse or on the course, golfers support each other in the preservation of the illusion that the real world does not exist and that life consists of infinite rounds of golf to be played in the company of one's fellows. While the golfer seeks solace with his friends, the widow is left alone to seek solace within herself, and she is apt to think that this is not a fair way for her to be treated.

She is apt to think of getting even. She is apt to dream of sweet revenge. Unmindful of Bacon's warning that she who studieth revenge keepeth her own wounds green, she is more likely to think that the next time she spots a green she would like to rub her husband's nose in it, that given half a chance she would show him what being in the rough was all about. She is more apt to think that the next time she gets her hands on a club she might well be inclined to take a swing at you-know-who. She might even put him in irons and give him a spike or two, or she might be tempted to grip him by the neck, give him a whipping, and put some backspin on his balls. Innocent of Joubert's remark that revenge is the abject pleasure of an abject mind, she might contemplate the delights of torture, the joys of driving eighteen stakes into her husband's heart. She might dream of giving him a clubotomy but for the fact that he had got one already. She might revel in the quintessential ravishment of crucifixion. She could nail him, like Saint Andrew, to an X-shaped cross, and above his head write, "Hell hath no fury like a . . ."

She could hang him by the pro shop for all to see, and listen to the grievous sighs of all the golfers gathered there, and watch their shaking heads, and listen to their sad laments that she hadn't even shouted, "Fore." But such lurid introspection only teaches the widow the truth of Milton's dictum that "revenge, at first though sweet, bitter erelong back on itself recoils"; revenge of a wrong only makes another wrong. To forgive a wrong is the best revenge.

I, too, had learned it was futile to challenge the wisdom of the ages. Granted, I had often indulged myself in little fantasies of throwing Don off his game by having him paged by loudspeaker from the pro shop while he was in the middle of a drive. I had thought of sending out scouts to track him down on the course to tell him that the *Mem Sahib* was in need of him. I had contemplated leaving him stacks of messages in the pro shop suggesting that he should come home PDQ. I dreamed of having him paged every ten minutes in the lounge. I had even thought of taking another whirl at the game myself and giving Don minutely detailed descriptions of my each and every round, until I realized that, if I were to adopt this plan, I would have to become a golfer—a brainwashed, spellbound wreck of a man who willingly admits to having a handicap so that he may chase a little, white ball. Clearly I didn't qualify. Occasionally I had longed to hook Don up to "Iron Byron." I had even made the association of the shepherd and the cross, but I had vowed not to be the one to give the game its first martyr. I would not make Don a hero. I would not be the one to create another golfing legend.

Besides, I was now happy with my lot. Through my vengeful study of the human soul I had arrived at a self-knowledge that years of analysis could not have brought. I had learned to turn loneliness into solitude and to make resentment into contentment. The children were growing more independent every year, and I could see that I had a life of my own to get on with. The new addition to our house was nearly complete. The foundation was poured, the walls up, the subfloor down, the roof shaked. I had only to finish the exterior siding, plaster and paint the walls, and lay the carpet. The electricians were coming to finish the wiring for the computer terminals, and once that was done I could get started on my research. I was about to become actively involved in job creation—my own.

I perceived that the type of analysis I had made from my observation of golf could have a much wider application. What I had done for golf I could do for sport. To this end I was anxious to get started on a treatise on *The Numerology of Sport and Its Practical Application for the Team*. I could envision a day when the trained numerologist would be employed as a regular member of the professional team's staff—a day when he or she would be as important as the team trainer, the team physician, the team psychologist, or the equipment manager. I was convinced that after the conclusion of my researches and the publication of my thesis, players and numbers would not be conjoined on a haphazard basis, but rather upon the scientific principles I hoped to establish. I even had dreams of new colleges built specifically for the training of the sport numerologist. I could foresee the day when sport numerology would be as hallowed a discipline as sport medicine. Perhaps in later years I could do some pioneering research in the field of number pollution. But for the moment I was pleased. Until two weeks ago I was happy that the universe was finally unfolding as it should.

When Don turned our 1979 beige Chevrolet Monte Carlo with the wire-spoke hubcaps into the parking lot of the Chimo Club and wheeled us into the parking spot reserved for the vice president, I no longer felt defensive and ill at ease. I was happy for Don that he had found a home. I was pleased that golf had given him a goal in life. I was glad that he still had something left to shoot for. Through the years the terrors and mysteries I associated with the club had disappeared. I no longer noticed the surplus of grey heads ensconced there. Each successive year I found the membership seeming younger and more full of vigour. Each year at the annual salmon barbecue I recognized more and more faces. The ones I didn't recognize I had probably talked to on the phone. I could even count on four fingers the number of pros that I had seen come and go. For me the only enduring mystery left to ponder was the transformation of the sleek, young radical I married into the rotund, greying VP I now live with.

As rumours of Don's presidency grew, I looked forward to the extra time that this would give me for my research. I felt like the proverbial pupa about to emerge from her chrysalis, about to spread her wings and fly. Then, two weeks ago last Sunday, Don returned home from the club unusually early. I went to the front door to see who had driven in. To my surprise it was Don. He was sitting in one of the deck chairs on the porch.

"Have a seat," he said to me, indicating that I

should sit down in the lawn chair adjacent to his on the porch.

"I've been doing a lot of thinking lately," he began. I looked at Don intently, my interest piqued.

"Believe it or not, I seem to be losing interest in golf. I've achieved everything I ever hoped to on the course. More, actually. I never thought I'd be a seven. And at times the arthritis in my fingers gets so bad that I can hardly hold my club. But that's beside the point. I've begun to think that we should spend more time together as a family. After all, here we are living on one of the most beautiful inland waterways in the world. We'd be crazy not to take advantage of it. I'm thinking of buying a boat."

This astounding statement proves yet again that the winds of change blow even on the golf course and through the clubhouse. Even a golfer changes. However, whether or not a golfer can become a yachtsman remains to be proven. The changes in myself are less discernible to my eye. Nonetheless, even I have mellowed enough to confess that one twilit night I discovered the secret of the proper swing. In sum: it's all in the breath.

About the Author

Patricia Jean Smith was born on Mother's Day, May 11, 1947, in Edmonton, Alberta. After spending the first ten years of her life on the prairies, her family moved to northern British Columbia. In 1969 she received a degree in political science from the University of British Columbia. Here she met her husband, Ron. They travelled to England, where he received his master's degree in English literature while she worked at the Gem Super Discount Store. During this time abroad they travelled throughout Europe.

After returning to Canada, Ms. Smith resumed her studies and in 1973 received a master's degree in comparative religion from the University of British Columbia, writing her thesis on the literature and philosophies of ancient India. At different times in her life she has earned a living as a lifeguard, swimming instructor, bath attendant, tea packer, legal secretary, social worker, and part-time teacher. Throughout her life she has been an avid sports fan, and was a member of the 1966 Canadian Junior Women's National Basketball Champions, the Marpole Queens. At present she limits her physical exercise to twenty minutes of yoga a day. She suffers from a severe case of baseball fever.

Her husband Ron golfs, writes, publishes, and teaches. They have two children: Nicole, aged eleven, and Owen, aged six.

Ms. Smith's first book made the finals of the first Seal Book competition for first novels by Canadians. She is currently working on her second book of satirical humour.

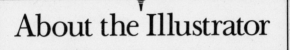

About the Illustrator

Trish Turner is a cartoonist who lives with her husband and two daughters in Lantzville on Vancouver Island in British Columbia. She is best known for her humorous greeting card line "Trish Lines."

TRISH TURNER
ILLUSTRATOR, CARTOONIST

TRISH LINES
Site 18, Box 35, Lantzville,
B.C., CANADA, V0R 2H0   (604) 390-4388